MOUNTAIN BIKING

The Skills of the Game

MOUNTAIN BIKING

The Skills of the Game

PAUL SKILBECK

The Crowood Press

First published in 1994 by
The Crowood Press Ltd
Ramsbury, Marlborough
Wiltshire SN8 2HR

British Library Cataloguing-in-Publication Data

A catalogue record for this book is available from the British Library.

ISBN 1 85223 802 X

DEDICATION
This book is dedicated to Chris Shaw,
who built many fine mountain bikes.

Picture Credits
Principal photographer Dave Stewart. All other photographs by Phil Gillam and David Yates, except the photograph of the author on page 6 (Thomas Edgar), Fig 4 (Rough-Stuff Fellowship), Fig 6 (*Mountain Biking UK* magazine) and Figs 88 and 89 (Garry Tompsett)
Line-drawings by Annette Findlay

Frontispiece: a fully suspended bike with oversize aluminium tubing making light work of a steep drop-off.

Acknowledgements
In particular I would like to thank Phil Gillam for his determined effort getting the majority of photographs ready for this book, and Phil Blacker and Andy Plews for their willingness to model for photographs and Paddy Blacker for generously providing the Newlands Studios for us to use. I am also grateful to *MTB Pro, VeloNews* and *Mountain Biking UK* magazines and Steve Thomas for allowing me to use some of their material.

Typeset by Avonset, Midsomer Norton, Bath
Printed and bound in Great Britain by BPC Hazell Books Ltd
A Member of The British Printing Company Ltd.

Contents

Involved with biking since childhood, Paul Skilbeck raced mountain bikes in 1988–90 before going on to coach and manage an elite junior team in 1991. He was appointed training consultant to the GB mountain bike team in 1993, and is a founder member of the British Mountain Bike Federation, for which he is presently co-ordinating the development of a governing body award for mountain bike instructors in England.

He is a full-time journalist, his range of experience covering most aspects of the cycling world. In recent years he has worked on the international racing circuit, and currently writes a training column for the internationally acclaimed cycle racing magazine, *VeloNews*.

For as long as I can remember, Paul Skilbeck has been heavily involved in the UK mountainbike scene. As a rider, coach and journalist he has accumulated an immense amount of knowledge and this book is a worthy testament to his expertise in all areas of mountain biking. I found his treatment of training and fitness in particular to be one of the most informative, accurate and practical I've come across in MTB publishing. Even those of us who have spent years in the saddle will find numerous gems of knowledge within the covers, and I have no doubt that it will give readers a solid grounding in the practicalities and theories of mountain biking.

Dave Smith
International mountain bike training consultant

One of the most important things about instructional books is the presentation. Paul Skilbeck effectively combines words and pictures here to highlight the key points in a range of essential skills and other aspects of mountain biking. The advice on equipment is based on his years of experience reviewing cycling products, and this section should remain relevant for years to come.

His first-rate all-round experience is evident in the common sense opinions offered to riders planning expeditions, and his time spent as an instructor has doubtless contributed to the way he selects valuable advice and the clarity with which he passes it on.

Closest to my heart are the racing and training chapters. In these he offers a wealth of practical information in just a few pages. I have no hesitation in recommending this book to mountain bikers at all levels of experience, as everyone stands to gain something by reading it.

Ned Overend
Seven times US Champion and 1990 World Champion

Introduction

What is it that makes the mountain bike, with its fat tyres and stout frame, so popular? The answer has several parts to it. It is because the mountain bike has something for everybody, it is stable and easily controlled, it is comfortable, it has excellent brakes for safety, and it has a wide selection of gears that makes pedalling easy on most terrains. Further, the handling qualities and the gearing afford the rider wide access to beautiful and exhilarating countryside rides.

In addition to these features the reassuring sturdiness of the mountain bike gives it a wide appeal, and the range of choice available in accessory components and frame design makes the mountain bike world a realm of possibility for the enthusiast as well as the casual user. Most important of all, mountain bike riding is fun. Excited, flushed faces are no less common amongst experienced riders than newcomers after a ride in the woods. One ride and you're hooked – perhaps that most accurately accounts for the enormous global popularity of the mountain bike.

Like mountain bikes, this book is for everyone. Its main aims are to help you choose the most suitable equipment, and how then to keep that equipment in good working order; to learn all the essentials of off–road riding skills; and to plan and prepare for more adventurous

Fig 1   Mountain biking is safe cycling for young riders.

rides. The chapter on racing, in addition to my own advice as a mountain bike training consultant, offers readers the experience and opinions of leading cross-country and downhill racers from the MTB World Cup circuit.

Although it is aimed more at beginner and improving mountain bike riders, the analysis of skills and riding position and much about racing will be of interest to more advanced riders, as will be the information on expedition riding.

7

Fig 2   Mountain biking is an activity for all the family.

THE ORIGIN AND DEVELOPMENT OF THE MOUNTAIN BIKE

The mountain bike gained international popularity in the 1980s, a time when we thought anything possible and were looking for new ways to achieve it. Unlike some other practices of the 1980s, mountain biking has proved a lasting success.

Off-road cycling is hardly a new activity. For example, in Britain a group of riders called the Rough-Stuff Fellowship has a tradition that dates back to 1955 of adventurous cycle rides, aboard conventional touring cycles on countryside paths.

Mountain bikes, however, have brought a new attitude to cycling – not only in the countryside, but in towns and cities also, all over the world. The mountain bike has brought adults back onto bicycles as well as attracting newcomers to cycling. People everywhere seem to want to ride mountain bikes.

There is no single inventor of the mountain bike. Many individuals are hailed as its inventor, but in all likelihood the truth is that it just evolved, true to the old adage 'form follows function'. Americans point to a nineteenth-century adventurer, Thomas Stevens, who rode around the world some hundred years ago on a vehicle resembling the modern bicycle. He must have done plenty of off-road riding, like it or not! A bike made for the purpose was the German 'Adler Mountain and Valley Bike' of 1949, fitted with three gears. Then there were the bikes ridden by Britain's Rough-Stuff Fellowship. They were also built for the purpose, but none of these examples sparked the off-road cycling boom.

Fig 3   Members of the Rough-Stuff Fellowship rode bikes to remote parts of Britain years before mountain bikes were invented.

The events leading to the mountain bike boom took place during the early 1970s in Marin County, California. It was in the hills just to the north of San Francisco that the modern sport of mountain biking had its beginnings, and it may never have happened if not for the wile of the wives of wealthy Los Angeles residents last century. These women bought large tracts of hilly land and used it for country walks and horse riding – it was their own space. They paid for it with their own dowry money, thereby guaranteeing that the land could not be developed in case it caught the business eye of their husbands. Through the outdoor activities of these women, the area gained recognition as a recreation ground.

The land has since been redesignated a watershed, and it now stands as an undeveloped tract of hills just across the bay from one of the world's major cities. During the 1970s these hills, dominated by Mount Tamalpais, inspired in a group of young open air enthusiasts, the same craving for adventure and love of nature that must have influenced those women to purchase the land in the first place.

Joe Breeze, Gary Fisher and Charles Kelly were influential amongst the pioneers of the mountain bike as we know it. In the early 1970s members of the Velo Club Tamalpais loaded heavy, single-speed bikes with back-pedal brakes and balloon tyres into the back of pick-up cars and drove to the top of Mount Tamalpais. From there they would charge down the fire roads on these 20kg 'ballooners', as the bikes were called. A day of racing down this long descent was enough to burn all the

9

grease that lined the back-pedal 'coaster' brake, so it would need to be repacked before further use. This led to the naming of the first known mountain bike race – the Repack Downhill – which was held on the side of Pine Mountain near Mount Tam.

As well as the need for better brakes, getting back up the hill was also on the minds of these riders. In 1974 a bike with a rear derailleur, five-speed freewheel, thumb gear shifters, triple chainwheels, motorcycle brake levers, and quick-release seat pin was built for the purpose. It was given the name 'mountain bike'. In 1979 the first production mountain bike was made, and the spirit of invention that led to its creation has continued to inspire many experimental designs since.

Mountain bike manufacturers exhibit a need to innovate with design and material. The constant flow onto the market of new, and generally better, products since the invention of the mountain bike has resulted in lighter bikes that can cover more terrain with greater safety and efficiency.

Milestones in product development have been Hyperglide gear shifting, SPD clipless pedals and Rock Shox front suspension. All of these technological

Fig 4   Britain's Dave Hemming at speed on a banked corner.

developments have increased the use and functional efficiency of mountain bikes. Rear suspension has been successfully integrated to the concept of a lightweight bike, and oversize aluminium tubing has contributed to a whole breed of lightweight frames. Lately, carbon fibre and metal matrix composite materials have suggested exciting possibilities, but thus far the light weight and smooth ride of titanium have made it the premium tubing material.

Frame geometry became steeper in the early 1990s then slackened a little as riders searched for the best combination of traction, pedalling efficiency and bike handling. Only two parts of the bicycle have so far defied the certainty that someone, some time soon, will come up with a design that is more robust, lighter and more functional: the chain drive and the triangular, tubed frame. For the demands of mountain bike riding, the mechanical efficiency of these is hard to improve on.

USE OF THE STUDIO GRID PICTURES

One of the most important things that distinguishes the skills of mountain bike riding from other forms of cycling is the need constantly to make subtle weight shifts in order to keep the bike moving as smoothly as the rider can over sometimes rough and undulating terrain. Other forms of cycling do require weight shifts similar in principle to those used in mountain biking, but in mountain biking the importance of weight movement on the bike is *critical*. For this reason the movement of the body in relation to the bike, captured in pictures of field demonstrations, has been replicated in front of a grid in a studio. The position of the bicycle in the studio remains static from one skill to another. The reader is thus able to see (by comparing grid shots of different skills) exactly how far the rider moves in given directions to perform a range of skills.

The purpose of this is primarily to assist the rider in estimating the degree to which he should shift weight on the bike to negotiate different ground formations successfully when out on the trail.

SUMMARY

In only a short space of time the mountain bike has come a long way, not only in its development but also in gaining a more widespread acceptance as a legitimate means of transport, sport and recreation. The mountain bike and its many users are, now more than ever before, the subject of study and learning at all levels.

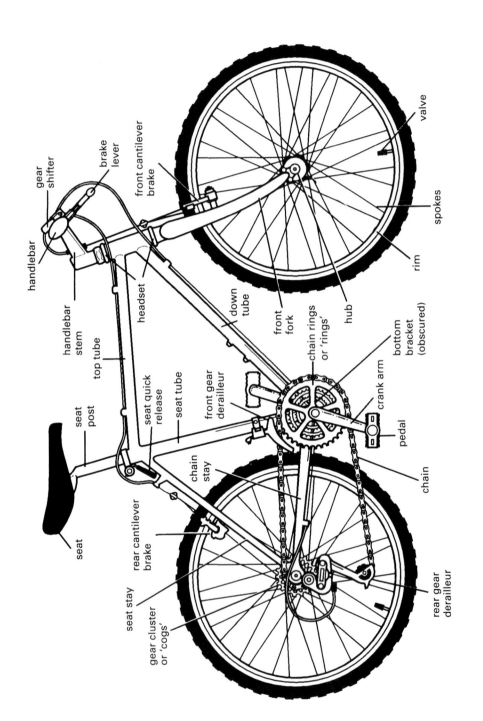

Fig 5 The anatomy of a mountain bike.

1
How to Buy a Mountain Bike

Buying a mountain bike can be very confusing. So many different makes and models exist, it can be difficult to decide between them. One of the great things about mountain bikes is that they are versatile machines that can be used for many different types of riding. It is at the lower end of the price scale that the most significant advantages can be gained by spending more.

Going to the right sort of shop will remove most of the chance element from mountain bike buying, and the most reliable way to find a good mountain bike shop is to ask a mountain bike enthusiast or consult one of the many specialist magazines. I read in a cycling magazine about a customer who queried the loose fit of a helmet he was buying for his son. He was told not to worry by the sales assistant, because when the child started cycling around he would get hot and his head would expand to fit the helmet! This would be humorous but for the critical importance of using a close-fitting helmet. It shows the lengths that sales assistants in disreputable shops will go to in order to make a sale. Do be cautious when making a purchase, and once you have found a good shop, keep your custom there.

As a rule the best shops have a range of very expensive bikes as well as one of cheaper models. This is a sure sign that the shop serves the discerning enthusi-ast market, which demands a knowledgeable sales staff. There are exceptions to this, however, so it is wise to talk to the shop staff before deciding where to buy. Yet even in good shops the customer needs to be well informed, and reading this book will help!

Part of satisfactory buying comes from going to the shop at the right time, which is when it's not too crowded, so you will find considerate and well informed sales staff who can give you their undivided attention for as long as necessary. Assistants who actually ride mountain bikes are often the best able to help in choosing a suitable bike.

The most important factor is size, and a good dealer will be reluctant to sell a bike that has not been tried by, and fitted to, the prospective rider. Two frame dimensions need sizing: height and length, or the seat tube and the top tube.

To size for height, the rider straddles the bike about half-way along the top tube. When the bike is the correct size a gap of 7–10cm will remain between the top tube and crotch. Sizing for length works like this: a rider with a long back takes a bike with a long top tube; a rider with a short back takes a bike with a short top tube.

A bike that doesn't fit well is not only a hindrance, it can be a danger. If a rider is worried about growing out of a bike too quickly, two things are worth considering. Firstly, a top tube that is close to the groin presents greater potential for injury in that area of the body in case, for example, the rider slips forward from the seat on a bumpy descent. Secondly, it's not difficult to sell a bike on the second-hand market.

MODEL

Although second-hand bicycles are cheaper than new ones, you should only make this kind of purchase if you have expert knowledge of bicycles or you know someone who can give an expert examination. It is all too easy to end up with a crash-damaged bike or one that is in need of costly repairs. Having said

that, there are many excellent second-hand bargains available.

The choice of a new bike may be between a few different ones in a price range, all of which fit and are appropriate for the rider's needs. In this case there's only one sensible solution – ride 'em and see! If the shop has a hire fleet, a range of different bikes can be ridden off-road. Otherwise test-riding must take place on the streets. This can still convey to the rider a like or dislike of the feel of the bike. There's nothing mysterious about liking the feel of the bike, and some bikes fit some people better than others.

Firstly, and most importantly, you should ask yourself whether the bike is comfortable. The seat height is easily

Fig 6   General-purpose mountain bike, most suited for touring or commuting.

Fig 7 Full-size wheels on a small frame. A bike this size is made for people around 150cm tall.

adjustable, but what about the body? Is it too stretched out or cramped up? Does the bike respond predictably? Lean it into a corner and see how stable it feels. Give it a few good hard pedal strokes and feel how willing it is to accelerate. After having test ridden a few bikes, the reader will start to get a clearer idea of what feels right.

If you want to test-ride a bike, you should bear in mind that it is not un-usual for dealers to ask for a substantial security. A lot of bikes are not returned when only small sums of cash or invalid credit cards are left.

A light, nimble feel to the handling is very important if the bike is for off-road use. Such bikes flick easily through cor-ners, but all the while they feel as if

they're on rails. If the bike is mainly for urban road use, comfort and visibility are most important. These two are often provided by a relatively upright torso position. For off-road touring a combi-nation of the three is good, but make sure the frame has eyelets for mud-guards and racks.

Mountain bike frames are consider-ably stronger than conventional and hybrid frames. If you plan to tour with panniers, you should always choose mountain bikes over hybrids, even though the wheel size of a hybrid is arguably more suitable. The extra sta-bility of the mountain bike when approaching hairpin bends with fully laden rear panniers makes this option far safer.

15

FRAME MATERIAL

Different frame materials will be encountered. Aluminium frames are generally lighter, but they have a rather harsh ride that tends to suit heavier, stronger, riders. Steel frames are more springy and these have proven popular over the decades with all types of rider. These are the two materials most likely to be offered, and there are many different grades of each. (Detailed information on the subject of steel and aluminium alloys can be obtained from back issues of the MTB magazines and books listed in Further Reading.)

At the upper end of the market carbon-fibre composites and titanium are priced well above even the finest steel and aluminium frame sets. Carbon fibre offers light weight, low corrosiveness and has good spring. Tubular carbon-fibre frames were popular during the early 1990s but some major manufacturers refused to use the material in tube form due to its tendency to snap in extreme crash conditions (for example, being hit by a car), where metals tend to fold up. This remains an issue of some debate in the industry, although present manufacturers claim catastrophic failure is not a problem often associated with the material.

The one-piece, or monocoque, design appears to be the way forward with carbon-fibre composites, but designers are still in the process of finding the best design for mountain bike use. This is in contrast to metal frames, which – save suspension – have not changed significantly in design for over a century.

Suspension is radically altering the design of the mountain bike frame. It allows the biker to ride faster downhill, and over bumpy terrain otherwise unridable. In addition, scientific research suggests that fully suspended bikes require less energy to ride over rough terrain than partially or unsuspended bikes. Suspension is already the norm on high-performance mountain bikes, and manufacturers are constantly making refinements to the frame and suspension unit

Fig 8 Front suspension, handlebar ends and sporting geometry: good for either racing or recreation.

Fig 9 Elevated chainstays remove the incidence of both the chain slapping against the frame, and being drawn up into the narrow gap between the chainset and bottom bracket.

design to improve what already works very well.

Titanium is great if you can afford it. Since the arms industry started to go into decline, titanium producers have been looking to open up new markets, and titanium is getting cheaper. Titanium 3/2.5 alloy, drawn rather than rolled into tubes, is commonly regarded as the best form of titanium. The material is lightweight, absorbs shock well, and is very slow to corrode. My opinion is that titanium offers the best ride of all mountain bike materials. If I could afford it, I'd have a titanium mountain bike.

The frame is the part of the bike that

Fig 10 Oversize aluminium, box section rear-end and front suspension: a high performance racer.

Fig 11 Full suspen-
sion. This design
has won the down-
hill World
Championships, but
it is also light
enough for cross-
country racing.

you will probably keep the longest, so make sure you get a good one first time round. Occasionally bike frames are built out of track. You can tell this by looking carefully from a metre behind the bike. If, when the back wheel is vertical, the front wheel is at a slight angle then the frame is out of track. Slight divergences make virtually no difference to the handl-ing, but if you have to choose between two bikes, this check may help you decide. While you are scrutinizing the frame, check the paint around the tube joints. If it is smooth, the joint is sound, but if there are pin-prick holes in it, the welder may have missed a bit! Fortunately, this is another rare occur-rence, but it is worth looking out for.

Fig 12 A different
version of the fully
suspended bike.
There are numerous
other designs.

18

Fig 13 Simple but classy: an off-the-peg frame from a custom builder.

CUSTOM FRAMES

Custom-made frames are frequently the most elegant, combining smooth, flowing lines with the highest manufacturing standards. Perhaps most importantly, riders with longer than average legs or torsos can get a perfect fit with a custom-made frame. For serious off-road work, a well-fitting frame reduces the risks considerably.

For example, I stand about 185cm and I have a long torso. When riding steep descents, on most bikes I have to put my hips well back from the seat – an undesirable option if the bike stops suddenly against a rock or tree root. Thus, frame fit has become a safety issue, as I must consider the possibility of bruising to the abdomen or even the groin.

What I personally need is a bike with a long top tube and a relaxed seat tube angle. I have tried simply fitting an ultra-long handlebar stem to a bike with average top tube but that compromised the steering control, so it was not the best option. For safety as much as riding pleasure, I need a bike with a very long (24in) top tube, but stock builders rarely make such a long reach, and certainly not in conjunction with a 19.5in seat tube (my size).

Problems also exist for people with very short torsos and long legs. They have to reach so far forward to the handlebars that it must be a major effort to put much weight on the front wheel – a must for several manoeuvres.

These examples are included to show just two practical reasons why custom frames may be chosen to suit a multitude of special requirements. Many

19

Fig 14   Inside a custom builder's workshop.

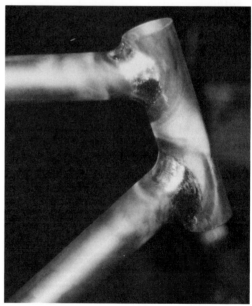

Fig 15   A custom frame lined up on a jig ready to have the seat stays brazed on.

Fig 16   This type of brazing is called fillet brazing. In this process a fillet of metal is built up around the tube joint. Before painting, the fillet is filed to a smooth finish, as shown.

Fig 17 A finished frame, painted to the customer's order.

people buy them to have a completely individual bike, or purely for aesthetic pleasure. A custom frame will be more expensive than a mass-produced one using an equivalent material, but people who are prepared to spend the extra money do not regret it.

EXTRAS

Having decided on a bike – and it's worth taking time over that – essential extras should be considered. One extra that warrants special mention is a method of binding feet to the pedals. Toe clips make a huge improvement to pedalling efficiency, and they prevent the foot from being dislodged from the pedal on fast bumpy descents. However, they do take some getting used to. The rider must become accustomed to wiggling the foot a little and pulling it backwards to remove it from the pedal.

Riders who have no problems with binding the feet to the pedals often decide to upgrade to clipless pedals. These are God's gift to cyclists. Clipless pedals lock the feet onto the pedals (you can disengage with a firm flick of the heel), and they further increase energy efficiency and safety over toe clips in many situations. Clipless pedals are expensive and require special shoes with a cleated sole to fit them. But amongst serious mountain bikers this is the universally accepted system.

Other accessories worth investing in are a good U-lock, lights, cycling gloves, cycling shorts, a jersey with pockets, pump, toolkit and a good helmet. The latter should be ANSI or SNELL approved. Lastly, serious riders might consider a cycle computer, which gives information about distance travelled, speed, and so on.

2
Basic Riding Positions and Techniques

What is the best position to adopt when riding your bike? The stretched-out, forward-leaning position of the adventurous recreational, or racing, bike is achieved by putting a big horizontal distance between handlebars and seat. Although common amongst experienced off-road mountain bikers, it does not suit everyone. Nevertheless, it remains as arguably the most versatile position. The photographs show two riders of quite different shape on the same bike. Although sizing is important, there is still a fair degree of flexibility in the definition of a safe riding position. The author, shown in Fig 18, would benefit from a slightly longer top tube. The model, shown in Fig 19, would be better fitted on a bike with a fractionally shorter top tube. The handling character-

Fig 18 The author has a long back. This locates the head, shoulders and chest further forward, as it does the centre of gravity. This has an adverse effect on the ability to ride steep descents but aids front-wheel control on steep climbs.

Fig 19 The model is 7cm shorter than the author, but by lowering the seat height, he is able to ride the same bike. As his legs are long for his height a safe gap will separate the top tube and his crotch when he stands straddling the bike.

istics of this bike may be perceived very differently by these two riders because their centres of gravity when seated are located in different positions.

In the past I have used my racing mountain bike for all types of use: racing, touring, commuting, courier work, the lot. On the other hand, a friend of mine who is a mountain bike instructor in the Pyrénées prefers a very upright posture on a bike with a short top tube and handlebar stem, and a small vertical gap between seat and handlebars – a position favoured by some commuters. When riding together on the steep, tight tracks of the Pyrénées we both made it down at much the same pace, but my friend's position turned out to be less efficient, for aerodynamic reasons, for flat sections of riding.

Theoretically the upright position is more efficient for climbing, in the sense that the rider's weight is more over the pedals, but this is complicated by the fact that on very steep climbs an upright position and short top tube make it virtually impossible to keep the front wheel on the ground.

Cycle couriers use mountain bikes a lot. The sturdy wheels and frames are well suited to the pot-holes of city roads, and with smooth tyres they become very swift machines. The cycle courier fraternity adopts the full range of body positions – from horizontal back to relatively upright – all for the same purpose in the same environment.

The biomechanics of mountain bike riding are more complex than they are for skiing or weight-lifting. For general-purpose mountain biking it is incorrect to say one body position is always better than another. The final decision on riding position should come down to personal preference. However, there are certain standards that have gained common acceptance because they suit most people. Ideally individuals will think about the particular dimensions of their body – such as arm length, leg length and torso length – and start making fine adjustments accordingly. A good reason should underlie any changes made to position. You should have a good idea of what you are aiming at and why you want to change.

Once a change has been decided upon, for example raising the seat because your legs are too cramped, it should be introduced over a period of weeks. If you ride every day, and you want to raise the seat a total of 4cm, this should be done in eight increments of 0.5cm, spread evenly over a four-week period. The reason for this is that the human body doesn't always accommodate sudden change. A different riding position, particularly seat height, alters the load placed on specific muscles and joints. Rapid changes could result in a sudden overload, and a soft-tissue injury in the knee or pelvic area is often the result. Gradual change allows the muscles sufficient time to adapt to a different load.

The standard body positions that are commonly accepted in mountain biking are set out in the following section.

LEGS

When the pedal is at its furthest point from your hip joint, the rider's knee should be slightly bent. If you are unsure whether the seat is too high or not, a helper should stand behind and watch you pedal – backwards if necessary. If your pelvis rocks while pedalling, the seat is too high. The ideal seat height for efficient pedalling is at the adjustment just below where the pelvis starts to rock.

PEDALLING POSITION

With or without a shoe fastening, only one foot position makes any sense for general balance and energy transfer. That is with the ball of the foot directly above the pedal axle.

PEDALLING ACTION
(Figs 20–23)

There is a most efficient way to pedal. Over the course of a day efficient pedalling will make a big difference to the number of hills that can and cannot be ridden up, and also to how much energy is spent. First the rider must be prepared to pedal with the balls of the feet using a rolling action, rather than flat-footed. The easiest way to imagine this is to think of climbing a stair case: you push off your toes. The other key to efficient pedalling is to think about pedalling in circles. Note from the photograph sequence how the rider's

PEDALLING ACTION

Fig 20   Good ankle flexibility is needed at this point, where the heel snaps down, and the toes drive forward. The ball of the foot drives down.

Fig 21   Here the ball of the foot is driving hard down and the rider has just started to pull the foot backwards. Style varies in this phase of pedalling. Some riders point toes down, others go heel first. Our model has taken the middle line.

heel moves up and down in relation to the pedal axle.

I recommend that, for all but extremely steep or exposed riding, mountain bikers use clipless shoe fastening devices. The main drawbacks are that they are expensive and take a few days to get used to, but for the enthusiast mountain biker they are generally safer and far more efficient than any of the alternatives.

The following instructions will be of most use to riders using pedals with a clipless fastening. If you use pedals with toe clips, try to follow the instructions, but beware of pulling your foot out on the up stroke. Riders using no fastenings can focus on the ankle articulation in the photo sequence, but will not always be able to direct force as described.

1. Starting at the top of the stroke, the toes are driven forward into the material at the front of the shoe. At this point the heel will come down quickly, perhaps even to below the toe.
2. As the foot moves down through the stroke it should be pushed hard down. The foot angle will be roughly level.
3. Fractionally later, the rider begins to pull backwards on the pedal. The heel will come up at the nadir of the pedal stroke.
4. As the pedal returns to the top of its stroke the leg pulls up and back. The heel will be much higher than the toes.

Fig 22   At this point the rider has almost finished pulling back and starts to pull up on the pedal. It is important to think about lifting the heel.

Fig 23   The effort of pulling up on the pedal will be felt in the calf muscles. The transition to the foot position in Fig 20 will be made with a quick, deft, movement.

This action is called 'ankling' and takes many hours' practice to master, but it is worth practising from day one. One thing that riders say takes time to get used to is the feeling of pushing forward and down with one foot while at the same time pulling up with the other.

By using ankling, more muscles in the leg are utilized. This not only relieves fatigue on the major muscles, it also brings more muscles into use on steep sections where it can be 'all hands to the pumps'. In addition to these points, ankling allows a faster, smoother cadence, or pedalling rate. This is also commonly regarded as increasing efficiency. As a rough guide, aim to pedal at 80–90 revs. per minute (where one rev. = a full turn of one crank arm).

HEAD AND EYES

The competent cyclist seldom looks at the bike when making routine control actions, such as braking or gear changing. The more you keep your head up and eyes forward, the better your chance of handling what you are about to ride over. Occasionally it is necessary to glance at the rear-wheel gear cluster to check on which cog the chain is, or perhaps to check the cycle computer or an unusual noise, and so on, but generally the rider should train himself to know where everything is on the bike without looking.

For off-road riding the chin should be up and the eyes looking some fifteen metres ahead. If you keep your head down off road, and you are not using a Crud Catcher, you will get a face full of mud from the front wheel. On road the focus of the eyes very much depends on the changing traffic and road conditions.

BACK

Many experienced cyclists, with thousands of kilometres clocked up, have poor posture. Rounded shoulders and arched spines are common, but unnecessary. Often this comes from riding with the seat too close to the handlebars. If the handlebars are sufficiently far from the seat and you train yourself to maintain a flat spine right from the start, postural problems won't arise.

The back should be kept still when pedalling. Bobbing of the torso and shoulders means that energy is being wasted. The most skilled mountain bikers appear to glide over the terrain, arms and legs working in precise co-ordination and the torso quite still. It isn't a tensed posture; it's actually very relaxed. You should not try to force it upon yourself, rather suggest it to your body as you ride.

3

Beginners' Off-Road Handling Skills

There are four core skills that new-comers to mountain biking should learn to gain a basic control of the bike. These are gear control, brake control, body weight movement and cornering basics.

Gear and brake controls are mounted on the handlebars and are designed to be instantly accessible. Experienced riders take advantage of this quick access to make rapid and subtle changes to both pedalling and rolling resistance. Beginner riders cannot expect to exercise such finely tuned control of the gears and brakes because much of the skill required lies in the rider being able to read the terrain accurately.

The first goal with the gear and brakes should be to acquire automatic control, where the operation of shifting gear or braking demands very little attention and so allows the rider to concentrate on other things, such as preparing for changes in the terrain. Complete new-comers to mountain biking can best get a feel for gear change and braking in a flat, open area where the terrain demands little attention. When familiar and confident with these two types of control, the rider is ready to go out on the trails.

GEARS
(Figs 24–26)

Chapter 8 discusses the merits of different types of gear changers. Here, the principles of gear selection are outlined. The diagram details the drive train. The three larger cogs are individually called the chain rings, or 'rings' for short. The cluster of smaller cogs attached to the back wheel, collectively called the gear, or sprocket, cluster are simply referred to as 'cogs'.

Broadly speaking there are two common types of gear shift control. The first, of which a few permutations exist, uses two levers for each control, while the other uses just one lever. Whether the fitted levers have a twin-lever action, or are the single-lever thumb shifters, the main principle of gear selection remains the same: a big ring at the front and a small cog at the back are for fast flat and downhill riding, and a small ring at the front and a big cog at the back are for slow uphill riding. The middle ring is used for a wide range of riding conditions in between.

Push-pull gear levers are located under the handlebar. The thumb pushes a lever to select a larger cog or ring; the index finger pulls a lever to select a smaller cog or gear. Thumb shifters are

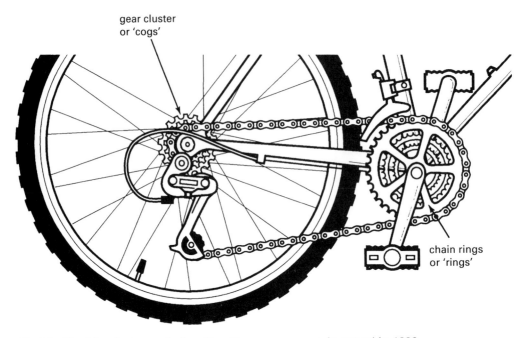

gear cluster
or 'cogs'

chain rings
or 'rings'

Fig 24   The bicycle transmission. Derailleur gears were invented in 1899.

the original mountain bike shifters and are mounted on top of the handlebars. They are the simplest and most reliable mechanism, but they are not as quickly accessible as the under-bar shifters.

Most new bikes made for serious off-road use are sold with under-the-handlebar gear levers, but the thumb shifters are more robust and durable. For this reason club racers and expedition riders often choose them in preference to the quicker shift type.

In order to shift the chain between cogs and rings the rider must keep pedalling. The technical skill in gear changing is in timing the shift so that the pedal cranks come to the vertical position fractionally after the lever has been manipulated. Timing the gear shift with the pedal stroke is more important when changing from a small to a large cog than the other way around.

Smooth shifting minimizes stress on the chain when it is derailed from one cog to another. Newcomers to mountain bike riding are normally surprised by how easy it is to twist or snap a chain by getting a gear change wrong, so it's well worth learning a smooth change. A snapped chain is a reliable way of spoiling an afternoon of mountain biking fun.

Changing gears on the front cogs is performed with the left-hand control and the rear cogs with the right-hand control. Changes on the front cogs make a big difference to pedalling resistance, whereas the rear cogs are used for a finer adjustment.

As a general guide to gear selection for different terrain, the middle ring and big cogs are used for short, very steep climbs that require some power over a short distance. On long steep climbs

Fig 25 Mid-1990s handlebar controls (above); Fig 26 Late-1980s handlebar controls (below).

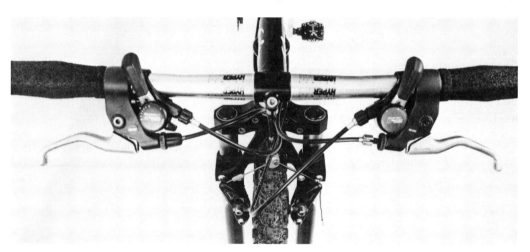

most riders would use the little ring (also known – with respect – as the 'granny ring'), and a big cog. Off road on flat gound the big ring is rarely used except in racing. Generally, the big ring is used for downhills. It is not that pedalling is always necessary on downhills, but using the big ring helps increase chain tension. In turn this helps to keep the chain from falling off the chain rings as the bumping forces cause it to flap up and down. Downhill racers sometimes use as many as three extra devices to hold the chain on the big ring, one of which is featured in chapter 8.

Another word about use of the gears, the chain should not be subjected to too much lateral strain. This means that the full potential number of gears available should not be used. For example, when the chain is on the big ring, it is advised that the two biggest cogs are not used.

Conversely with the granny ring, the two smallest cogs should not be used. When on the middle ring, don't use the biggest and smallest cogs. When riding, the mountain biker should glance back to the cogs to see how many are left before the chain is put at risk. This may sound like extreme caution, but seven- and eight-cog gear clusters, along with the grit and grime of off-road riding, amount to more abuse than a chain can take.

BRAKE CONTROL

As with gear shifting, it is wise to find a good open space to get used to brake control.

First, make sure the brakes are correctly adjusted. The tip of the lever should travel about two centimetres before the pads contact the rim. The brakes should never be adjusted so that the lever can touch the hand grip, but allowing some play in the lever gives more feel to the braking action and gives the rider a stronger grip on the brakes.

The front and rear brakes have very different effects. The front brake stops the bike faster. It is worth bearing this in mind in order to avoid nasty moments. At a guess, 70 per cent of braking is done with the front brake, so you should not be afraid to use it, but you do need to get a feeling for how hard the front brake lever can be pulled before the rear wheel leaves the ground. When this is prac- tised, it should be done progressively over a few attempts so the back wheel lifts just a few centimetres at the most.

While the front brake is the primary tool for washing off speed, the rear brake plays a more subtle role, being mainly used to add to the overall braking

and balance the decelerative forces of a slowing front wheel. However, it is also sometimes used to move the rear end of a moving bike to one side or the other.

In some downhill situations the front brake is best avoided. Examples of such situations are as follows:

1. If it is very steep and bumpy.
2. At the point the rider needs to turn the front wheel on a steep slope.
3. At ground contact after the front wheel has been in the air.
4. When travelling very slowly on a steep slope.

If juddering is experienced in the forks and handlebars when the front brake is applied, it means the brake pads are toed out, or incorrectly adjusted. (*See* chapter 9 to find out how to toe in the brake pads.)

The back brake will lock up the back wheel if applied hard. Get a feel for this on a gravel car park or in a place where a bit of skidding won't cause ecological damage. Out on the trail it is normally advisable to avoid locking up the brakes. There are two reasons for this. Firstly, it leaves ugly marks on the ground, which damage the soil and flora structure. This is not only an act of destruction; it also makes mountain bikers unpopular with other land users. Secondly, the rider is often in fuller control when the wheels aren't sliding. Admittedly changing direction with a controlled slide is a useful technique, which is covered in a later chapter, but it does not give the mountain bike rider licence to tear up the trail where that is not necessary.

A technique for braking control fre- quently used by mountain bikers is called 'feathering'. Used in a wide range of situations, from high speeds to low speeds on steep and gentle gradients, it is simply a very fine modulation of the brakes. This is a very useful technique to adopt right from the start. It involves repetitive, yet gentle, pumping of the brakes so that speed is washed off in small measures. Grabbing at the brakes probably causes more crashes than not using the brakes at all!

The 1993 USA Women's Downhill Champion, Penny Davidson, puts braking too hard in the wrong place high on the list of mistakes she tries to avoid. The fact that a rider at that level should even consider making such a mistake shows the high degree of precision involved in correct modulation of the braking force.

To get the general impression of how brake modulation works, think about driving a car; dab the brakes here and there to keep things smooth and flowing, but stamp on the brakes and not only do you waste energy but sometimes the result is a nasty surprise. It's the same with mountain biking, only a mountain bike is easier to crash than a car.

GRIP
(Figs 27–29)

Use of grip is an essential element of safety and control. When on downhills or undulating terrain, it is very common for riders to rest one or two fingers on the brake levers, even when there is no immediate need for them. Many of the pictures in this book will show the rider with fingers poised over the brakes but not actually pulling the lever. One of the main reasons for this is to eliminate the need for a sudden hand movement if braking unexpectedly becomes necessary. Grabbing at the brake lever can result in a less controlled braking action, and it certainly increases reaction time. For these two reasons riders are advised to cover the brake when descending or on bumpy terrain. This notwithstanding, whenever possible the rider should keep his thumb wrapped securely around the hand grip when covering and squeezing the brake lever, likewise when shifting gear if possible.

With thumb shifters, as illustrated in the photographs *(overleaf)*, the thumb must unwrap from the bars to change gear, which can be a disadvantage of this type of gear shift control. It is sometimes very bumpy on the trail and getting a hand bounced off the handlebars frequently precedes a crash. If it is very rough, many riders will keep the thumb and index finger wrapped around the grip, using just second, third and sometimes fourth digits to squeeze the lever. Perhaps most common is for riders to grip with the thumb, third and fourth fingers, braking with the first and second digits. A one-fingered grip is often used for feathering the brakes.

I suggest trying several combinations. In high mountain ranges the rider can sometimes descend for over thirty minutes. The work the forearm must perform on long, rough descents can fatigue muscles controlling the braking fingers. On such descents switching the combination of braking fingers can help to retain an element of control if the rider refuses to stop for a rest. Such extreme conditions are not the place to try out new ways of using the brakes. Learn a wide repertoire of braking grips and continue practising them on easy terrain.

31

GRIP

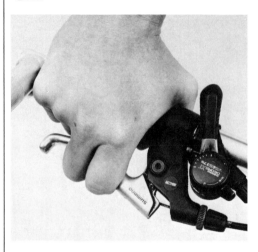

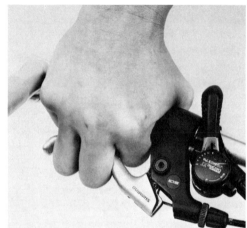

Fig 27 *(Above)* Two-fingered grip – the most common combination, it gives strong braking force.

Fig 28 *(Above right)* Two-fingered grip for exceptionally rough terrain; the braking force is not as strong as fig 27.

Fig 29 *(Right)* One-fingered grip for feathering the brakes.

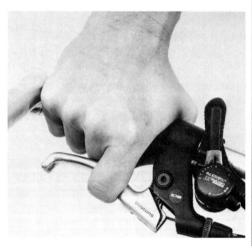

BODY WEIGHT MOVEMENT

Much of the control in bike handling comes from moving the body in relation to the bike. Normally in off-road conditions the rider is performing weight shifts every few seconds. These may only be subtle shifts, but subtle weight shifting is the essence of good mountain biking. By learning fine control you will give depth to your repertoire of skills.

To start getting a feel for fore/aft weight shift, while still in the open space used for gear shift and braking exercises, the first thing to do is to stand up on the pedals, knees slightly flexed, while the bike rolls along slowly. In this position your limbs should feel springy, not stiff

32

or floppy. From here move slowly forward to place a lot of weight on the hands, then move slowly back so that the hips are well behind the seat and the elbows are almost fully extended, remembering to keep that spring in the joints.

Trying this again, but not going so far forward or back, you can then attempt to lift the rear wheel when in the forward position and the rear wheel when in the backward position. To lift the rear wheel, flex the knees a little more than for the first exercise, then do two things at the same time:

1. Grip the bars firmly and rotate the wrists forward.
2. *Gently* spring forward and up on the pedals, pointing the toes down and pushing the soles of the feet backwards.

This skill takes practice, and you should be careful not to launch yourself over the handlebars and to keep your feet in contact with the pedals.

Lifting the front wheel is a lot easier. With the weight now shifted back, pull up and back on the handlebars. Again, the rider should attempt this action gently at first because overdoing it will result in a fall backwards off the bike.

What has been described involves gross weight shifts. Finer weight shifts are used momentarily to unweight the front or rear wheel, and they account for the spectrum of body positions in between the two above.

In many cases weight shift can be effected while being poised on the seat. All that is necessary to pass smoothly over a small bump, for example, is to get up a few centimetres and back from the seat a little. Pull up and push forward on

the handlebars as the front wheel goes over. Then remain off the seat a little to prevent buffeting as the back wheel rises over the bump. You are simply taking weight off the wheels and the seat at the right time. For sharper bumps lift the front wheel more vigorously and spring up on the pedals to lift the back wheel over the edge.

CORNERING BASICS
(Figs 30–32)

I recommend learning about cornering while travelling at a moderate speed. Cornering at low speeds is more difficult and feels very different. High-speed cornering demands considerable experience.

'Weight the outside foot, lean the bike, push forward with the inside hand'. These words from Penny Davidson comprise the advice she gives herself for fast but tight corners on downhill courses. However, some extra points are worth considering when learning the technique of cornering.

It is a technique that requires a fairly standard set of movements to start it going. The golden rule in medium- and high-speed cornering is 'Don't turn the handlebars.' The leaning action of the bike will do that for you. Of course, you must also be careful not to prevent the handlebars from turning. The main steering control comes from leaning the bike, articulating at the hips, and pointing the knees in the desired direction.

Newcomers to the sport can take a while to come to terms with the notion of turning the front wheel without making an effort to turn the handlebars.

33

The critical mechanics of bicycle steering can easily be observed if the rider walks along beside the bike with one hand placed on the seat. To make the bike go straight, it must be perfectly vertical. If the seat is pulled gently to the left, the bike will lean over and the front wheel will change direction. The bike will move to the left. The same applies with steering to the right.

The classic cornering style is shown in Fig 30 and can be learned using the following sequence:

Setting up for the Corner

1.   Leave the outside pedal at the bottom of the pedal stroke.
2.   Tilt the handlebars and lean the bike into the corner.

In the Corner

The bike will now be turning, and you will not have consciously turned the handlebars.

1.   Put weight on the inside hand.
2.   Move the inside shoulder forward and over the outside hand.
3.   Feel the articulation, in the pelvic region, between the line of the seat tube and the line of the body. This feels a little bit like leaning over to the outside of the bike.
4.   Stand heavily on the outside pedal.

Coming out of the Corner

1.   Bring the handlebars back up to the horizontal.
2.   Resume pedalling.

If you still have trouble getting the feel

Fig 30   Balanced position with good traction. In this position the rider will feel as if leaning against the corner. Note that he is slightly out of the seat. This has three functions: (1) it puts more weight on the front wheel; (2) it puts more weight on the outside pedal; (3) it gives a smoother ride.

of the classic cornering style, try riding along in a straight line and then lean the bike over. See what it takes to retain the bike on a straight course while still leaning it. Stop doing this, and the bike will automatically turn.

Once you have mastered those core skills, you can apply them in many situations to improve your cycling.

CORNERING

Fig 31 Pedalling through a corner. The corner follows a short, steep descent. In slippery ground the tyres are not giving good lateral stability. The rider has delayed his turn until meeting a natural berm. This not only gives better traction, it also gives the rider more time to get into position.

Fig 32 The rider has started his turn too early. The ground is slippery, and he compounds this by putting his weight too far to the inside of the bike. At the point this photo is taken, he is well off-balance and is unlikely to recover. Note that his position is not far removed from that of the rider in Fig 31.

DOWNHILLS
(Figs 33–34)

The grid pictures show clearly how far the rider has moved in relation to key points on the bike, namely the handle-bars, the pedals and the seat. Note that the pedals are approximately horizontal in relation to the ground and that the heel of the front foot is just below the toes. The rider has come up off the seat to allow himself to move back and also to absorb bumps better. It is not a very steep slope, so the crotch has come back

DOWNHILL TECHNIQUE

Fig 33   Observe the position of the hips: a little way off the seat and a little way back. His weight is evenly distributed between the pedals and his arms are poised.

Fig 34   The rider is looking several metres ahead to the ground onto which he will shortly ride. His body is athletically poised in case a sudden movement is required.

just a few centimetres past the rear of the seat. This brings the rider's centre of gravity to just behind the mid-point. The knees and elbows are almost fully extended but have – from force of habit – some spring in them. Note that the chin is well up. This is because the hill is not very long, and the rider is surveying the flat ground he is shortly to ride onto, having already checked that his path down the slope is clear.

If it appears the rider's body is tilted excessively forward in the photographs, this is the position adopted by the majority of mountain bike enthusiasts. It is a very stable position, which keeps the centre of gravity as low as possible.

DITCHES AND GULLIES

Crossing open gullies is a skill that beginner mountain bikers who have been active in other outdoor sports should be capable of learning right from the start. The most important thing is to practise this only in dry gullies. If the bottom is muddy, the front wheel could bog down, which would probably send the rider sprawling.

Riding the Gully
(Figs 35–40)

Notice how the rider approaches from wide, using the full width of the track. This means that the bike travels down the slope as close to the vertical as possible. While this tack increases the decelerative forces upon climbing the opposite bank, it reduces the risk of a wheel wash-out either on the way down or up.

Although the slope is actually steeper than the one in the previous photograph, the rider does not get so far back on the bike. This is because he must very soon make a big forward shift, so he stays as far forward as he can.

The general weight shift in this sequence requires the rider to move quickly from back to forward, and the timing of this move is critical. If he moves too soon, he will not get past the bottom of the gully. If he moves too late, he will risk the front wheel climbing into the air. The thrust forward is only brief, and by the time the bike is emerging from the gully, the rider has almost fully regained his normal riding position.

RIDING THE GULLY

Fig 35 Approaching the gully.

Fig 36 The rider is still in a neutral position on the bike.

Fig 37 A backward weight shift and slight recoil of the back help to absorb the sudden shock of hitting the gully floor.

Fig 36(b)

Fig 37(b)

Fig 38   With a muddy wall approaching the rider quickly starts his forward move. Note he is still pedalling.

Fig 39   The rider continues to go forward, countering the angle and backwards force coming through the bike. He is in a low gear, and quick pedal strokes make him highly responsive to the changing slope.

Fig 38(b)

Fig 39(b)

Fig 40 Moving back onto flat ground, the rider takes care to put in an extra pedal stroke to get him over the lip of the hill, and as the bike starts to accelerate he is able to return to the seat.

Running the Gully
(Figs 41–43)

Riding through gullies is fun for those who can do it, but it is not compulsory. The alternative is to walk or run through. In situations like this the bike is a hindrance if left on the ground, so it is better to carry it. Note that the model in the photographs actually keeps the bike at the same level as the path. This means he spends less energy getting back up the other side.

CLIMBS
(Figs 44–45)

People who know nothing about mountain biking think getting one of these bikes up a hill is simply a matter of pointing it at any gradient and pedalling. The truth is soon revealed when out on the trail.

Three things commonly cause a moutain biker to dismount when going up hill: it is just too steep; the back wheel slips; the rider loses balance so puts a foot down and can't get started again. The basic climbing posture is illustrated in the photograph sequences.

RUNNING THE GULLY

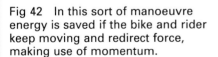

Fig 41   Even though he decided to climb off the bike, the rider has still approached the gully from a wide angle. This will make sure the rear wheel does not drag in the weeds as he completes the turn. Also, by keeping the bike's angle at 90 degrees to his shoulders, he will have to worry less about balance. Note that his right foot is passing inside his left ankle as he dismounts.

Fig 42   In this sort of manoeuvre energy is saved if the bike and rider keep moving and redirect force, making use of momentum.

Fig 43   After an efficient passage through the gully the rider has enough momentum to make it easily up the other side.

CLIMBING POSITION

Fig 44   The rider has moved a long way forward, countering the forces pulling his front wheel up. These forces come from tilting the front wheel up and the rider pulling up and back on the handlebars. Note the foot position on the pedal. The focus of view is closer than it is for descending, but the rider must remember to look ahead for obstacles and line choice.

Fig 45   Climbing on a loose surface requires careful steering control.

The surface consists of large pebbles, which offer considerable resistance. Therefore, the rider has to make the most of each pedal stroke. This is made evident by looking at his heel, which is well beneath his toes at the bottom of the pedal stroke. Getting the heel down is not unusual in situations like this, although not all riders would choose this pedalling technique.

The rider has also moved a little way forward on the seat. This he has done partly to keep the front wheel on the ground and partly to add force to his pedal stroke. If he moved much further forward it is likely that his back wheel would start to slip. This is an important point in climbing: finding a balance between keeping the front wheel on the ground and weighting the rear wheel sufficiently to prevent it slipping.

Note also the use of the arms. With elbows flexed, the rider is able to make accurate pulling movements on the handlebars. When timed to coincide with the down thrust of the pedal, this momentarily helps the rear wheel to gain traction.

On very steep climbs it is difficult to control the steering, especially when pulling back hard on the handlebars. In this situation the rider should look ahead for the line that looks as if it will allow the easiest passage for the front wheel and enough traction for the back wheel. If it is extremely steep, and the rider is uncertain about making it to the top, it is better to dismount while still in control. Grinding to a halt on a steep hill is often followed by a long tumble backwards. If the rider does grind to a halt, he should put on the front brake and lean forwards onto the handlebars. If a fall is inevitable, don't fight it: go sideways.

GEAR SELECTION

Once the basics of gear selection have been mastered, you should think about strategic use of gears – which gear to use for the prevailing conditions. What, for example, if you approach a sudden and short but very steep hill?

If you wait until half-way up to change into a really easy gear, the gears won't work: they only change effectively when there is a very light load on the pedals. On the other hand, if you select a really easy gear well in advance, you will not have sufficient momentum to make it up the hill. The answer is to change the chain across two or more cogs (with the rear derailleur) at once. Do this right at the bottom of the steep bit after having taken a good run-up.

If riding on a forest track, where distant visibility is not good and the terrain is undulating, it is better to stay in a gear that is very easy to pedal. If you suddenly encounter a steep hill, even if it is only five metres high, being stuck without momentum and in a big gear will prevent you from climbing that bump on the bike.

Even the world's leading mountain bike racers ride in gears that are easy to pedal. Not only does this put less strain on the connective tissue in the legs, it also gives better control over the bike.

CARRYING THE BIKE
(Figs 46–47)

As any mountain biker will admit, there are hills that cannot be ridden. In this case, you will have to carry your bike. The photographs illustrate two of the more common methods of carrying a

43

TWO METHODS OF CARRYING THE BIKE

Fig 46 The two-armed portage can be good on long climbs and keeps the bike more clear of the ground.

Fig 47 Carrying the bike this way, the rider has greater freedom of movement and can reach out for support or assist striding with the free arm.

bike over long distances. The first method employed is useful for elevated-stay designs or for some rear-suspended bikes, where the elbow cannot be passed through the main triangle while the hand is grasping the top tube. The second method involves doing just that. Then with the top tube resting on his shoulder the cyclist has moved his hand to grasp the handlebar. This holds the bike firmly to the rider, and one hand is left free to do as it pleases.

4

Getting Adventurous

One of the lasting joys of mountain biking is that the more skills riders have, the more they can do and the more they can enjoy the sport. The skills covered in this chapter are useful in all situations, in both low- and high-speed riding, and in racing and recreational situations.

First, I would like to offer a few words on tactical gear selection. Riders who have gained the confidence to ride challenging uphills or blast through undulating terrain often start breaking rear derailleurs. This is not the fault of the derailleur; it is the result of a lack of tactical gear changing skills. Look at the rear derailleur. It is a flimsy design, and it will soon break if attempting three or four cog changes under a heavy load, but it will perform this function rapidly while the power train is smooth and the chain and cogs are moving quickly. Therefore, you must learn to anticipate the gear needed for a particular stretch and select that gear before the heavy load comes down on the pedals.

BUNNY HOP
(Figs 48–53)

Some obstacles do not warrant getting off the bike. Some of them can be cleared with a jump. This jump is known as the 'bunny hop' – an indispensable skill for any mountain bike rider. Not only is the bunny hop useful for clearing logs; it is also good for clearing drainage trenches and unwitting snakes that slide out onto the trail just at the wrong time.

CRASHING LOGS
(Figs 54–58)

There are times when the bunny hop is too difficult to employ (for example, on a steep downhill), but the rider cannot, or chooses not to, slow down for an obstacle, such as an erosion or drainage trench or a log across the trail. In these cases, it is often sufficient simply to heave the front wheel over the obstacle and then unweight the rear wheel, without initiating a hop. A common mistake that riders make in trying this is to unweight the rear wheel too much and so be leaning too far forward as the rear wheel bounces over the obstacle. The back end normally kicks up hard over such an obstacle, and if the rider is too far forward, he will be propelled over the handlebars. Note that sharp-edged obstacles will normally cause snakebite punctures to the rear tyre when this manoeuvre is performed.

Junior World Championship Downhill silver medallist, Dave Hemming, explains a similar technique, the 'rear-wheel hop': 'Pedal until you lift your front wheel. Then, as soon as you see it's

BUNNY HOP

Fig 48   Approaching the hop the rider pushes down and forward on the handlebars. Note the crouching position on the bike.

Fig 49   To lift the front wheel, move back on the bike and pull up with the hands.

Fig 50   Spring up off the pedals, pulling the rear wheel with you. With clipless pedals this is easy, but with toe clips or flat platform pedals, the rider will need to push the feet hard back against the pedals for grip.

Fig 51   The rider pulls his legs up under him to get good rear wheel elevation.

Fig 52   The rider again bends the elbows to help absorb the impact of the front wheel landing.

Fig 53   As the rear wheel comes down the rider lifts a little out of the seat to help absorb the shock.

Fig 48

Fig 51

Fig 49

Fig 50

Fig 52

Fig 53

CRASHING LOGS

Fig 54 The exaggerated position the rider assumes is because the frame on his bike is longer and has front suspension.

Fig 55 Crashing logs involves an action very similar to that used for the bunny hop.

Fig 56 The rider does not pick up the rear to the same extent as he does for the bunny hop. In effect he just unweights the rear wheel.

over and the back one is about to hit [the obstacle], push it forward. This lifts the back one and pushes the bike forward. Don't do it too early or you'll fall off – it's all weight shifting.' That one takes some practice.

ULTRA-TIGHT RADIUS TURNS
(Figs 59–61)

Sometimes, on narrow tracks, it just is not possible to ride around in a 180-degree arc and face the other way, and some hairpin bends are so tight that the back wheel will not follow the front around. In these situations it is useful to grab the front brake, lean forward so that the back wheel goes into the air and pivot the rear section of the bike, landing it in line with the front wheel.

This is not an easy skill to explain, so you need to use some imagination. Going downhill on a tight, narrow hairpin bend you should first turn the front wheel around the bend. Having done this, you should pull hard on the front brake and lean forward. The back wheel will automatically go into the air. From here it is mainly a matter of letting physics do its job. Provided the back wheel is allowed to go high enough into the air, it will come down fairly much in line with the front one. If you feel the back is going too high in the air, let go of the front brake and the back wheel will

Fig 57 The back of the bike rises into the rider's crotch. This is an impact he has to absorb. If he moves with it he could go too far forward and over the handlebars.

Fig 58 Finishing the manoeuvre.

49

ULTRA-TIGHT RADIUS TURNS

Fig 59   In order to pivot on the front wheel, the rider must get his weight well forward.

Fig 60   Balance, control and timing used correctly make this a relatively simple skill. It is largely a matter of the rider keeping cool.

quickly return to the ground. This is an easy-paced skill that requires no sudden or rapid movements and does not take a lot of practice to get right.

Rehearsing this skill on the flat, where gravity and gradient are not there to help, make it much easier when you arrive at that tight corner on the descent. The photographs give an idea of what the body should do. Note that the shoulders and arms remain relatively static throughout and that the rider's gaze is focused on one point. Keeping

the head still is the key to success in many balance exercises, this one included. Also, note that both brakes are engaged.

Tight Radius Turns
1. Stay relaxed and let it happen.
2. Keep your head still.
3. Experiment to see how high you can let your rear wheel go.
4. Sideways movement of the hips make the bike follow.

Fig 61   A sense of rhythm can help with the front-wheel pivot.

Track Stand
1. Fix your eyes on a point on the ground 2 metres ahead.
2. Feel for even weight distribution between your feet.
3. Get used to letting the rear foot go down.

TRACK STANDS
(Figs 62–64)

The track stand is all to do with delicate weight shifts from one foot to the other. It can be of use in many situations, especially where it is wise to stop but to put a foot down could make it difficult restarting, for example on difficult descents or on very rough ground where the rider needs to pause momentarily to check the route options.

Learning it is easiest done facing up a very gentle slope. Stand up on the pedals, which are horizontal. Shifting the weight to the outside of the bike, turn the handlebars into the slope. The forward pedal will be the one on the side to which the wheel is turned. Then rock forward, easing weight onto the forward pedal. The front wheel moves forward a few centimetres, and you then rock back, gently weighting the rear pedal. The bike then moves back. Repeat this. A master of this skill can take his shirt off while in the track stand position!

The principles of the track stand can also be used in getting around very tight corners. The technique here is to steer with the front wheel, stand up on the pedals and lean out and forward. The body position should look much like that in Fig 62 with the chin vertically over the front axle. Once the wheel is turned, steering is most effectively controlled by shifting the body weight and leaning the bike, not by turning the bars further.

The one thing you have plenty of in these slow manoeuvres is time, so relax and take it easy when learning and practising these skills. Riders who tense up normally fall off.

51

TRACK STANDS

Figs 62–64 The bike is not still for long in this exercise. It is normally rocking forward or back. Use of rhythm and feeling through the pedals are hallmarks of this skill.

TECHNICAL CLIMBS
(Figs 65–66)

The photographs show two different approaches to climbing. It may not look like it, but the first climb is close to the model's limit. The surface is slippery, so he must keep some weight on the back wheel. This he does by remaining seated, but he is also putting plenty of force into his pedal strokes.

In the second climb, his hips are almost vertically above the ball of his foot, which puts more weight into his downstroke. In order to keep the front wheel stable, his shoulders have come forward over the handlebars. This puts weight on the front wheel, which aids tyre traction. He has approached the hill with chain on the middle chain-ring and in the middle of the gear cluster. At the critical point, where the gradient suddenly steepened, he made a double shift (while the wheels were still turning quickly) off the chain, to the small ring and to a big cog. Also at this point, he started pedalling very fast and hard but did not lose his rhythm. The muscles only have fuel to power this intensity of effort for up to ten seconds. He was up the hill in about five, so it was all right!

On longer slopes, or those with more technical challenge – such as tree roots, ruts or rocks – your approach should be a little slower, at a pace you can maintain for several minutes.

Cadence and pacing are keys to making it up long slopes with plenty of technical challenge. The only way over some obstacles is with a maximal effort, but this can only be a very brief burst. If you are exercising above your aerobic limit, such an effort could be hindered. The reformation of creatine

Fig 65   The rider is further forward on the bike than in Fig 44. This is in partly in response to the increase in force he has to counteract in order to keep the front wheel on the ground and partly because he has moved forward on the seat to give himself a more powerful pedalling position.

Fig 65(b).

Fig 66 Professional racer Paul Hinton shows good balance and poise, ready to respond to any changes in terrain. Standing up on the pedals when on long ascents helps relieve the leg muscles used for seated climbing.

phosphate (which fuels maximal effort) is delayed in the acidic environment produced in the muscle when a rider is above his aerobic limit. Thus, any hill should be ridden within your aerobic limit in order to permit some brief, intense efforts.

While seated, much of the steering on long, steep climbs comes from the knees and hips, as the hands are assisting in the effort of power production. Using bar ends can be a help to put weight on the front wheel, but riders can expect to suffer from impaired muscle control on long, hard climbs if they have been above their aerobic limit. This is because the acidosis caused by anaerobic work temporarily decreases muscular co-ordination.

The eyes should focus on where you

want to go, not on what you want to avoid.

Fig 66 shows an important technical variation. By adopting the standing position, the rider gives himself an option to react quickly should the need arise. Note that he is using his bar end extensions. This will further increase his steering control by putting more weight on the front wheel.

The rider here is not in danger of losing traction, so he is easily able to stand on the pedals, but he still keeps weight on the rear wheel by keeping his hips low and fairly well back. Mountain Bike World Cup campaigner, Tim Davies, says of climbing out of the seat, 'You need to use a gear that is light enough to pedal but also big enough to get your front wheel off the ground for obstacles.

54

A bigger gear tends to dig your rear wheel in more, which gives you more traction.' This technique is more readily available to riders who are in excellent physical condition, as it gives the legs a lot more work, now having to support the weight of the body.

TECHNICAL DESCENTS
(Figs 67–69)

Fig 67 shows the most important part of riding a rooted, rutted descent: surveying it first and assessing whether or not it is ridable. On the day this picture was taken the roots were wet and slippery. The rider chose the line he would take, but then he realized he would have to apply the front brake going over the roots, so he opted not to ride it as the risk of a front wheel wash-out was too great.

Figs 68-69 show two different approaches to riding drops on steep slopes, both adopting the same position on the bike. In Fig 68 the rider has simply ridden over the drop, which has given him a steep bike to stay on. As long as his front wheel is not slowed by the brake or any obstacle, this is not a problem. The technique employed in Fig 69 is to keep the front wheel in the air as long as possible. If the rider can maintain this position, the drop-off effect is reduced.

One big problem the rider must overcome when on slow descents is that of front brake modulation. The front brake must be used if speed is to be kept to a minimum, but when turning the front wheel under the effect of braking it has a tendency to wash out if the surface is loose or slippery. Careful timing of

Fig 67　Knowing when not to ride prevents damage to rider and bike.

brake application is the answer.

The golden rule with steep descents is 'Never put both feet on the ground'. This is a very good way of initiating a broken collar bone. Nevertheless, when turning corners on steep descents it is sometimes a good idea to dab the uphill foot on the ground if necessary. If you are losing your nerve on a hill and want to put a foot down, the front wheel should be turned into the slope first. This will bring the back around and get the bike across the hill. It is then safe to put the uphill foot down. If it gets very steep and the descent is long, you will have to get so far back off the seat that your abdomen is positioned just behind the seat. The only problem with this is that if the bike is stopped suddenly by an obstacle, your abdomen will be buffeted by the seat.

55

Fig 68 Pulling the front wheel into the air over a drop-off is easier if accompanied by a pedal stroke.

Fig 69 The rider is not as far back on the bike as he gets for other purposes. A rider with a longer torso would push the hips further back, as would this rider if he were on a shorter bike.

The eyes should focus on where the rider wants to go, not on what the rider wants to avoid.

FAST DESCENTS
(Figs 70–76)

Riders on public land are advised to take it easy on descents. It may be fun to let rip, but it can be dangerous. A mountain biker travelling at 50kph could easily kill a young child. Legal and financial considerations aside, who would like to live with such guilt? Unrestrained riding on public land also gets bikes banned. The place to let go is in a mountain bike race. Many riders enter races not to finish high up in the results but to develop their skills and do some flat-out riding. It's well worth the entry fee.

Top-level cross-country racers say that line is everything in riding the descents, but that's only because they have all the skills required to make it down most hills. Downhillers would agree, but they might add that psychological preparation also counts for a lot. This section will focus on the physical skills of descending. (There is a mention of psychology in chapter 6.)

The position for fast descents is much as it appears in Figs 33 and 34: hips poised just above and behind the seat, elbows slightly flexed, pedals horizontal and eyes scanning the terrain three to five seconds down the trail.

The elbows and shoulders should act mainly as shock absorbers, but the wrists must keep the fingers tight on the hand grips. As stated in chapter 3, it is always worth keeping one or two fingers poised over the brake levers.

Braking during corners at high speed shows poor form. The rider should have anticipated the corner and braked before it, allowing a smooth passage through. Under brakes there is a far greater risk of losing traction through a corner. Also, if speed is reduced before the corner, the rider can actually accelerate through it, allowing a fast exit.

When encountering bumps on the descent, expert riders will normally skim over the tops, barely touching their

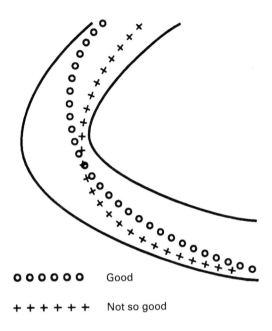

○ ○ ○ ○ ○ ○   Good

+ + + + + +   Not so good

Fig 70   Cornering line options.

brakes and barely touching the ground. Some riders find it helpful to accomplish this by gripping the seat between the inner thighs, moving the bike around as a unit with the body.

When approaching corners, it is necessary to break this connection and articulate at the seat. If the corner is preceded by bumps that go into the corner itself, brake before the bumps. It is not advisable to try and lose speed quickly in the bumps. If there is some flat ground in between the bumps and the corner, feather the brakes through the bumps and hit them hard before the corner on the flat ground.

SLIDING THE WHEELS

There are three places where one or both of the wheels will slide: on steep,

57

CORNERING OPTION ONE

Fig 71

Fig 72

CORNERING OPTION TWO

Fig 74

Fig 75

Fig 73

Fig 76

slow descents, on fast, dry descents and on fast, dry corners. Otherwise, wheel sliding should be avoided at all costs. Locking up the back wheel for the sheer joy of raising a dust cloud and scarring the earth just fuels the anti-mountain bike lobby. Unfortunately this lobby is far larger and more powerful than the mountain bike lobby, so there is no justification for giving it a valid reason to have mountain bikes banned.

Steep, slow descents can demand rear-wheel slides on tight corners. In amongst the trees, for example, where space is restricted and speed must be kept to a minimum, it can be very useful to feather the front brake and bring the back of the bike around quickly with a slide to set up for the next corner. There may not be the space to let it follow the turning arc around, or the grip to bring it off the ground, pivot, and land it safely.

Fast, dry descents can cause a bike to slide no matter what. At speeds of around 60kph, the bike leaves the ground very easily, even off bumps of just a few centimetres. At this speed the wheel will slide slightly on landing, before it starts rolling, like an aeroplane wheel. There is little the rider can do about this except know that it will happen and try not to worry about it.

You will need to let the bike go into a two-wheel drift on some fast, dry corners. You can get out of this by steering the bike in the direction of the drift, but that should not be necessary. If correctly timed, the drift will take the rider to the end of the corner, and accelerating away in a straight line will terminate the drift.

Getting into the drift can be a little difficult, as riders tend to be tentative and tense up slightly at the point where

REMOUNTING ON THE DESCENT

Fig 77   The rider steps forward to approach the bike. The rear wheel is not yet locked at this stage.

Fig 78   The rider steps up to the bike, placing the front foot vertically beneath the seat. The rear brake is then engaged and the wheel locked, and the bike pivots on the rear hub.

Fig 79   The rider positions himself astride and slightly to one side of the seat.

Fig 80   As the front wheel starts falling the rear brake is released as the rider moves further onto the bike.

Fig 81   The feet find the pedals as the front wheel contacts the ground.

Fig 77

the tyres cut loose and start drifting. Firstly, you must not have too much weight on the outside pedal. Secondly, the bike must be going at a considerable speed (so wear plenty of protective equipment when practising). It is largely a matter of just letting it happen after that, but if you want to encourage the sideways drift, you should inflate the tyres to around 60–70lb per square inch (4–5 bar). For all but the most skilful riders the two-wheel drift is only useful on wide trails, and it is certainly on these that you should practise it.

REMOUNTING ON THE DESCENT
(Figs 77–81)

If you have had to get off the bike on a descent, it can be a problem remounting if the gradient is steep. The technique shown in the photograph sequences may appear spectacular and flashy, but it is in fact one of the most practical and controlled techniques for a rapid re-mount while the bike is on the descent.

It is important to maintain a firm grip on the rear brake until the front wheel is on the ground. If it feels a little daunting at first, spend some time on a gentle slope getting used to it. This technique should only be used on clear slopes where the ground surface is relatively flat. If there are trees close ahead or the terrain is very bumpy, you will be running the risk of the front wheel jamming against an obstacle, which would probably lead to a fall.

Fig 78

Fig 79

Fig 80

Fig 81

5
Planning Expeditions

ACCESS TO OFF-ROAD ROUTES

Mountain bikes have restricted access to off-road countryside trails. Access restrictions vary from country to country, and in federal systems from state to state. Furthermore, agreements are constantly being set up between mountain biking authorities and land controllers about mountain bike use in sensitive areas. In view of this, you should check with the national controlling body for mountain biking to find out the current situation.

As a rule of thumb, horse and four-wheel drive tracks are within limits, as are those signposted for cycling use. Single-file tracks, or 'singletrack' are frequently out of bounds. Mountain bike riders should certainly not take access to the countryside for granted. Much of the access we once had has been rescinded, and much of what is left was granted on the condition that mountain bikers use it responsibly. Irresponsible riding jeopardizes the rights of all mountain bikers.

Professional opinion about mountain bikers differs. Some leading countryside recreation authorities regard mountain biking as something that many people wish to do, is potentially harmonious with other forms of land use and the environment and presents particular management challenges.

Other authorities, on the other hand, regard mountain bikers as a pain in the neck. Legally, we are skating on thin ice, as it is not difficult to bring down a ban on mountain bikes in an area of woodland or open space. Proof of this is the alarmingly large number of parks and paths that have been closed to mountain bikes during the past five years in most countries where mountain bikes are used.

If the sport is to reach its potential, the best way to establish mountain biking as a legitimate countryside recreation is by showing that we know how to use the countryside.

THE MOUNTAIN BIKE CODES OF CONDUCT

Several different versions of trail conduct exist. Two of them are outlined here, and they give the general picture of the sort of behaviour necessary if we are to continue to enjoy access to the trails.

The Union Cycliste Internationale (UCI) is the international controlling body for all forms of cycle sport. It has issued a code of conduct for mountain bikers all over the world. It is as follows:

1. Stay on the trail
   ride marked trails
   avoid footpaths
   read a map

2. Give way to horses and walkers
   make sure they hear you approach
   ride carefully when you pass
   split your party into groups of four
3. Be kind to birds, animals and plants
   and keep your dog under control
4. Avoid erosion
   skids show poor skills
5. Stay mobile
   wear a helmet
   take a first-aid kit
   carry enough food and drink
   pack waterproofs and warm
   clothes
6. Take pride in your bike
   maintain it before you leave
   take essential spares and tools
7. Be tidy
   take your litter home
   always guard against fire

H – Hydrates heavily
I – Indulges in ice cream
J – Jumps joyfully
K – Knows knobbies
L – Laughs long
M – Mails mud missive
N – Never negligent
O – Oils often
P – Protects parks
Q – Quibbles quietly
R – Rides reverently
S – Savours singletrack
T – Takes tea
U – Usually unhurried
V – Vicariously victorious
W – Won't whine
X – Excommunicates xenophobes
Y – Yawns at yahoos
Z – Zinfandel zone

An additional code of conduct exists which is far more esoteric but also contains some important messages. It is put out by a US-based organization called WOMBATS. This acronym stands for Women's Mountain Bikes and Tea Society. It is run for women, by women, but men are also allowed to join. WOMBATS has a worldwide network of members, all of whom subscribe to the notion of having a wild time on bikes without being imposing or showy, and there is a wealth of knowledge and wisdom behind its off-beat façade. Its 'Trail ABCs' reads as follows:

A – Adores adventure
B – Brings beloved bicycle
C – Coughs courteously
D – Decelerates demurely
E – Eyes exotic excrement
F – Feels fine
G – Gets grimy

PLANNING – SOME GENERAL CONCEPTS

Going out for a mountain bike ride takes forethought and preparation, even if you are just going down to the local woods. At the very least the necessary checks start with the weather report. If the weather permits a ride, you then need to wear and pack the correct clothing, pack a repair kit to save the nuisance of having to walk home, fill the water bottle with an appropriate drink to help lasting the distance and give your bike the once-over to spot anything that might cause problems on the trail (*see* chapter 9).

Every rider should be confident of completing the set course. If there is any uncertainty about the ability of all members of a party to complete a ride, contingency plans should be made to avoid anyone being left cold, exhausted and hungry out in the open. Pick a route that passes through villages where cafés and pubs are open, so that riders can reheat and refuel or telephone for assistance. Alternatively, identify an easy shortcut on a sealed road, but remember that riding up big hills is hard work – on or off road. Newcomers should build gradually but regularly from thirty-minute rides up to full-day rides, and then progress from there.

The following sections offer information about the sort of things mountain bikers need to be properly prepared for and equipped with for rides from two hours to several days in duration. The lists should be treated as guidelines only, and individuals may want to alter them as personal circumstances dictate.

An exhaustive equipment list does not exist. If you were equipped with everything that might be required in all conditions, you would be unable to manoeuvre your bike out of the garage! What many experienced mountain bike tourists have done at some point is to compile a list of everything they have carried on a trip and ticked off what was not used. This gives them a better idea of what will be necessary next time.

EASIEST RIDES

Beginner-level mountain bike riding is often well catered for in Forest Enterprise land and in Country Parks, although not invariably. Riders should check before making their first visit to a new place. Where provision is made for mountain bikes, waymarked trails are provided, making routes that range between thirty minutes and about half a

day. The signposts make navigation easy, and the tracks are normally well maintained and ridable. Maps detail the trails and are available at site offices. This type of riding can also be fun even for seasoned racing or touring mountain bikers who want a relaxed, easy mountain bike ride. The following might be needed on such a ride.

1. Helmet and leather-palmed gloves.
2. Wind/showerproof shell
3. Full water bottle
4. Basic toolkit
     4, 5, 6mm allen keys
     15cm adjustable spanner
     chain tool and spare chain links
     puncture repair kit (including frame-fitting pump, patching kit and tyre levers)
     spare tube
5. Money for snacks, phone calls, etc.

HALF-DAY RIDES

Weather watching is important to mountain bikers, particularly those going into hills or mountainous areas. The details of DIY weather forecasting are worth learning but are too involved to be covered in this book. You can, however, ring up the local met. office.

A half-day ride lasts up to four or five hours. To be confident of staying out this long and returning happy, you need to run through the following checklist for rides of easy to moderate difficulty.

1. Good basic fitness. This should not be your first mountain bike outing. If you are returning to the sport, it is especially easy to overestimate your current ability.
2. Check the bike is in good condition.

Fig 82 A basic toolkit for rides up to one day.

Fig 83 Rear pockets can carry the tools and other necessities on short rides.

3. Plan a feasible route and use an appropriate map (in Britain O/S Land-ranger and Pathfinder series maps). Use a recognized orienteering compass.

4. Get the best available weather forecast for the precise area to which you are travelling.

5. Take adequate clothing:
    helmet
    leather-palmed gloves
    wind/showerproof shell
    long-sleeved jersey
    polypropylene or similar undershirt

6. Food (e.g. trail mix, specialist energy bars, honey sandwiches wrapped in greaseproof paper) and a full water bottle. I recommend drinking every twenty minutes, even in cool weather and in between meals, and eating small mouthfuls every thirty minutes after the first two hours.

7. Simple first-aid kit.

8. Toolkit:
    puncture repair kit
    15cm adjustable wrench,
    8/10mm crescent spanner
    4, 5, 6mm allen keys
    chain tool
    crank puller
    spare tube
    spoke key
    2m copper wire
    two elastic bands
    10x3cm piece of canvas or similar
      (ripped tyre wall)
    rear brake and gear cable

9. Money. Take notes and coins.

10. Whistle (in case you need rescuing). The internationally recognized distress

signal is six blasts followed by a one-minute pause, then another six blasts. The reply is three blasts, then a one-minute pause, then three blasts.

11. Survival tin. This can be bought, or home-made using a tobacco tin. Include things like string, damp-proof matches, cigarette lighter, razor blade, safety pins, needle and thread, fishing hook and fishing wire, unlubricated condom (carries water), tea bag, sugar, two squares of chocolate.

12. Swiss Army knife.

All that may be a little excessive if the ride is taking place very close to civilization, but if the route takes the riders fifteen kilometres or more away from the nearest form of habitation these things can help an incapacitated rider to survive until help arrives, which might be a matter of days.

FULL-DAY RIDES

Full-day rides last from five to ten hours. Such rides tend to be very tiring, whatever level of fitness a mountain biker has, but a tiring ride is very different from an ordeal. An ordeal is what you will go through if lacking the basic training, health, or equipment. The planning and equipment list is similar to that for a half-day ride, but there are a few extra points to consider and items to carry.

Weather is of greater significance on a full-day ride than on a half-day one. If it is going to turn really bad up in the hills, you don't want to be there, even if you know the route off by heart. It is worth turning back if the weather appears to be going that way. If the weather has

already turned bad, and it starts getting worse, you should not press on regardless. Get off the high ground as quickly as is safe. This means it might be necessary to leave your bike behind if it is damaged and unridable.

You should also bear in mind that it's easier to become stuck in an isolated place on a full-day ride than on a half-day one, so make more of an effort to inform a responsible person of your anticipated route and return time.

The checklist for full-day rides is as follows.

1. Carry a survival blanket if going into a remote area.
2. Take lightweight lights in case of cycling the last few kilometres on road after dark.
3. Carry more food, and take some extra carbohydrate powder to mix with your water.
4. Roubaix-type leg warmers and an extra undershirt are all the extra clothing that you should need over and above what would be taken for a half-day ride.
5. If the bike passed the pre-ride bike checks (outlined in chapter 9) tools in addition to those in the half-day toolkit are not necessary.
6. Everything should fit into a hip bag and an under-seat tool bag, but if it doesn't, take a small backpack that hangs low on the shoulders (so it won't catch on the helmet) and which has a waist strap.

On a full-day ride you should expect and plan to take frequent snacks, say every twenty minutes, after the first two or three hours. Doing this will make all the difference in the final two hours of the ride.

GENERAL CONSIDERATIONS

Your equipment requirements will, of course, alter with the weather conditions. You should give a great deal of thought to your particular needs in specific riding environments.

Equipment

Thin tyres – 1.5–1.7in – are generally better for muddy conditions, as bikes tend to clog less than with wider tyres.

The chain is better lubricated with a heavier gauge lube in winter and wet conditions. A light lube is too quickly washed off, making the chain more prone to damage. In summer, it is better with a light lubricant and frequent cleaning. A heavy oil tends to attract too much dust in summer.

Terrain

In many countries the ground gets wet in winter. If ridden in these conditions, the mountain bike is going to get very muddy, so allow for much shorter rides which stay closer to civilization. Things have a greater tendency to break and suddenly wear out when it is wet and muddy. Also, reduced daylight hours should be considered in relation to departure time.

On the other hand, winter riding can be dry and clean if the ground is frozen, or other dry climatic conditions prevail.

Clothing

In summer, the only item of specialist cycling clothing I would strongly recommend in preference to normal clothes is a pair of lycra shorts. In winter,

I would advise the full cycling kit: overshoes, Roubaix tights, thermal tops, gloves, the lot. This type of clothing is so much less uncomfortable when it becomes muddy and wet. Also, it is less restrictive of body movement in all conditions.

Mountains

Hills are fine if there's no snow lying or forecast, but I don't recommend trips into alpine or hilly regions on bikes during winter. Snow clogging makes mountain bike brakes very ineffective. If the snow is dry, it can be fun to ride in it, but otherwise the problems with cold make mountain biking in snow downright dangerous. When cycling at speeds over 15kph, the wind-chill factor on a bicycle can become critical.

I once rode fifteen kilometres, on an icy road, up a valley in the Swiss Alps during early January. It was a steep, high-walled valley, and in the final ten or so kilometres sunlight did not fall directly on the valley floor, where the road was. On the way back down, the wind-chill factor made the cold intolerable. Despite travelling with the brakes applied and pedalling backwards as quickly as possible, my partner and I realized we were in danger of suffering hypothermia. Thus, we were compelled to stop every five minutes and spend two minutes performing exercises on the spot in an effort to keep our core temperatures up. (In the circumstances this proved to be the most effective action. However, had we been a long way from base with no food, that would not have been the case as we would have dangerously depleted our energy reserves.) It took us longer to get back down than we took riding up the valley. We would have needed bulky suits to have stayed warm on that descent, but they would have been a nuisance to carry on the way up. The simple answer is not to do rides like that.

Most experienced mountain bikers have some stories of unpleasant episodes where they made planning and management errors. Perhaps this is part of acquiring wisdom, in which case the best advice is to go off without a qualified guide only if you're certain you know what to do in emergencies.

Ski resorts aren't a safe winter option for mountain bikers at all. Taking a mountain bike to a ski resort and bombing down the piste is likely to endanger skiers and cause trouble with the mountain management. Unless you are really desperate to take your bike, outings should be on foot or skis instead. They're far more suitable for winter enjoyment of the mountains.

Fig 84   British path-finding ace, Gary Tompsett, prepares his bike for an overnight ride. He is able to carry all he needs with this compact lightweight equipment. Using a larger rucksack extends potential range limits substantially, but the weight of the rucksack can cause the cyclist pain in the lumbar spinal vertebrae.

ORIENTEERING EVENTS AND WEEKEND TRIPS
(Figs 84–85)

For weekend trips a bike will need to be fitted with a luggage rack, but if you plan to compete in a path-finding event, the rack can be dispensed with, although a map board should be attached to the handlebars for competition purposes.

The equipment you will need for orienteering events and weekend trips is much the same, except for one vital point. An organized event involves riding in a controlled environment where, if riders get into trouble, help and rescue are quickly at hand. Mountain bikers on weekend trips can get to very

inaccessible and remote areas, often unreachable by other land-going vehicles. This being the case, it is advisable to take extra food provisions and a comprehensive first-aid kit on such a ride. Riders who go on trips like this without a sound knowledge of – preferably training in – first aid are asking for trouble.

Appropriate food for such a trip would be lightweight and have good nutritional content. Dried potato, porridge oats, pasta and rice are all excellent. Packet soups and freeze-dried vegetables are also very good.

Frequent (every twenty to thirty

Fig 85   Handlebar set-up for a
path-finding event.

minutes) eating is recommended on this type of expedition. This need not be in solid form. Carbohydrate powders, which can be mixed with water, are easily available and are the most efficient form of energy intake. Dried fruit and nuts make good nosebag food. Between these foods, sufficient minerals, vitamins and energy are provided for the weekend. Powdered milk and tea or coffee are also easily carried, and they provide a good boost to morale when you are feeling worn out. Parmesan cheese is also very light and can add a lot of flavour to an otherwise bland meal. If you are not in a competition, why not also carry a few things mainly for the taste? Some cooked meat or tinned fish or a little chocolate for dessert are all possibilities.

Acknowledging Limits

The hardest decision is often the one to stop and get off, rather than ride a section. Close to home on frequently used routes, you can test your improvement by riding new, more difficult, sections. This is an essential element of skill development and one of the most thrilling challenges of mountain biking. On an expedition out in the wilds, the opposite is true. In remote areas you should stay within your limits.

MOUNTAIN BIKE TOURING

Off-road touring has degrees of

difficulty, but even the seemingly simplest routes should be approached with careful preparation and sound knowledge. Off-road touring is nothing at all like on-road touring; the latter is a breeze in comparison.

If you are planning a tour but have little experience of this form of travel, the first step is to complete several weekend trips, starting with mundane, less challenging routes. There is so much to be learned about mountain bike touring that building up a body of experience is the only way to gain sufficient knowledge to embark on an extended tour, confident about handling all the many situations that might arise.

The big difference between on- and off-road touring is that off road you must have the expertise to be self-sufficient in every situation and cannot rely on the good judgement of government surveyors as to what is an acceptable gradient for a wheeled vehicle to climb or descend.

The obvious mechanical problems that are likely to occur from constant vibration, bumping and rattling are only part of the problem. There are several demons. The off-road tourist should have a working knowledge of emergency treatment of fractures, concussion and CPR (cardio-pulmonary resuscitation). How to avoid heat-stroke and hypothermia is also essential knowledge, depending on the climatic conditions. Riders can be bitten by poisonous spiders, snakes or jellyfish so you should know how to treat such injuries, as you should those from poisonous plants, such as poison ivy or poison oak.

Good navigation and map-reading skills are also important – not only to prevent or remedy getting lost. Off-road touring in mountain ranges can involve climbs that take four hours or more. The descent may take more than one hour. Thus, there's only time for two mountain passes some days, and being able to estimate gradient in percentage terms from looking at contour lines on a map is important in planning the route. Compact books detailing this sort of survival information are available from specialist mountain sports shops, and they are worth reading before departure and carrying on tour for consultation if needed.

If this gives you the impression that mountain bike touring is a big undertaking, then the words have been effective. In its purest form, it is only for the most adventurous and dedicated rider. It certainly does not conform to the Council of Europe slogan, 'Sport for All'!

However, there are happily several alternatives that are more accessible. One is to try a tour on planned, tested routes with automobile back-up, run by a commercial company. For riders planning an entirely self-sufficient tour across really severe terrain, such as mountains, desert or tundra, it is worth putting plans back for a year and going first with a commercial operator across similar terrain. What you learn in a controlled environment could save your life when you are out on your own. Another of the more accessible forms of mountain bike touring is to plan a route that sticks to wide, frequently travelled trails. Doing this reduces much of the risk and guarantees the trails will not be too physically demanding.

One of the major differences from on-road touring is luggage carrying. Years of research and development have gone into providing reliable baggage equipment for road bikes, but off-road cycling presents a whole new challenge. It partly depends on the nature of the trails taken. A tour in the Pyrénées, for example, would not be practical on a bike with side-mounted panniers. The tracks are so narrow and the hills so steep that the panniers would often hit the uphill slope, causing the rider to be thrown off down the slope. Furthermore, the bikes must sometimes be carried long distances, which rear panniers make very difficult.

Alpine mountain bike tourists tend to use a set-up similar to path-finding eventers. Indeed, riding such events is good preparation for many of the challenges faced by the mountain bike tourist.

Rear panniers are only a sensible option where the intended route is known to be mainly on wide, well-travelled tracks. On wider trails front and rear panniers can be used, which allows the rider more time between food restocking stops. This can be very valuable on long, flatter journeys.

Another option, where a fair degree of mountainous riding is expected but with little need to carry the bike, is to mount two front panniers on the rear rack. Most front panniers are not as deep as rear panniers, so are less likely to catch on obstacles on and beside tracks. None the less, a backpack may still be needed.

Much of the conventional wisdom on luggage distribution needs to be rethought for off-road touring. Handlebar-mounted bags are subject to so much shaking that they don't generally survive longer than a week. Where full panniers are not advisable, you could consider carrying a front pannier with some weight on top of it. However, I have not tried or heard of anyone trying this option.

What you take on tour should be influenced not only by general precepts but by your experience. Equipment choices that are intensely irritating to one person may be perfectly acceptable to another. However, despite the importance and value of first-hand experience, off-road tourists are here offered a few hints which will be helpful on the shorter journeys used to prepare for tours of over one week in duration.

1. Use a superglue to fasten rack bolts and bottle cage bolts, and then carry spare nuts and bolts, and superglue.
2. Cut a couple of old inner tubes lengthways into long strips and pack them somewhere accessible. They make very effective ties and binders.
3. If going into a remote area, take a bike with a standard brazed steel frame. If the frame snaps, a welder can normally be found in the most far-flung of places. Aluminium and bonded frames require somewhat more specialist equipment for repair.
4. Shimano SPD pedals with the flat plastic platform accessory fitted to one side are the optimum in efficiency for alpine touring. The flat is used for steep traverses; the clip is used for climbing.
5. Make sure the rack fits the frame perfectly and doesn't slope back or forward. Sloping racks invariably cause the luggage to slide down the slope.

Mountain survival, safety and navigation skills have only been touched on here as they are detailed subjects which should be studied more thoroughly than is possible within the limitations of this book.

6
Racing and Other Competition

TYPES OF COMPETITION

Mountain bike competition, even if riders don't enjoy the racing, is still an excellent opportunity to do some flat-out riding without restraint beyond personal safety. Furthermore, many useful techniques can be learned by watching how the other competitors tackle obstacles, corners and hills. Several different forms and levels of mountain bike competition exist, and events cater for the entire population range: from local club events to international competition, in age categories from under twelve to over forty.

Two important things that distinguish mountain bike racing from other forms of cycle racing are a light-hearted atmosphere amongst riders at every level of racing, and the philosophy of self-sufficiency and resourcefulness. Riders are allowed no external assistance and so have to make their own mechanical repairs. If a bike breaks, the race is over for that rider – just as an excursion would be for a recreational rider out on the trail. In the interests of health and safety, the Union Cycliste Internationale (UCI) allows mountain bike riders in cross-country races to accept water replenishments and extra eye protection at specified points on the course.

The different types of mountain bike competition are cross-country, downhill, hillclimb, dual slalom, trials, enduro, and path-finding events.

CROSS-COUNTRY
(Figs 86–88)

The blue riband discipline of mountain biking, cross-country racing, is included in the Olympic programme for the first time in 1996, at Atlanta, USA.

Cross-country racing is an all-round test that includes handling skills, physical fitness and mental toughness, reading the terrain and finding the best line, fast repairs and resourcefulness, and making tactical decisions. It is the most accessible form of mountain bike racing for beginners, partly because of the large number of events organized over a wide area, but also because only basic skills are necessary for riders to enjoy completing the course. Many of the world's leading cross-country racers have converted from cyclo-cross racing, but others have come from mountain sports, cross-country running, moto-cross, and road cycling backgrounds.

Cross-country mountain bike racing takes place on signposted circuits,

Cross-Country – Men	
Category	Duration (hours/minutes)
Elite*[†]	2:30
Expert	2:00
Junior (16–18yrs)*	1:30
Sport 1 (19–25yrs)	1:30
Sport 2 (26–34yrs)	1:30
Veteran (35–44yrs)*	1:30
Masters (45yrs)	1:30
Super Masters (50yrs+)	1:00
Youth (14–16yrs)	1:00
Sprogs (under 14)	0:30
Fun (all ages)	0:30
Cross-Country – Women	
Category	Duration (hours/minutes)
Elite*[†]	1:30–1:45
Expert	1:00–1:30
Junior*	1:00
Sport	1:00
Veteran(30 yrs+)*	1:00
Masters(40 yrs+)	1:00
Youth	0:30
Sprog	0:30
Fun	0:30

Downhill

The race length is the same for all categories. The duration varies between up to twelve minutes in some American and European events, to under two minutes in some British events.

Categories are generally divided into men and women, and then junior, senior, and veteran. The same age limits as for cross-country racing apply.

N.B. At the time of writing, these figures were accurate for racing in Britain and for World Cup events. However, rules do change and discrepancies exist between nations. Therefore, it is best to verify these with your national federation.

* World Championships categories and classes.

[†] Olympic categories and classes.
Downhill is not an Olympic sport. World Championship categories and classes apply in both Cross-Country and Downhill.

Guidelines to Table 1   Mountain Bike Categories and Classes, and Race Duration

Fig 86   Man-vs-Horse-vs-Mountain Bike: a gruelling event held in Wales. A legal technicality, identified in 1994, presently bars mountain bikes from this event!

Fig 87   Mountain bike races can take the riders to spectacular locations.

Fig 88   The hectic start of a cross-country event.

normally varying between three and fifteen kilometres in length. It is not essential that the race goes over mountains; almost any tract of land can provide a worthy course, so long as it is ecologically robust.

Point-to-point races are another form of cross-country racing. They tend to be tougher than riding a circuit event, but they are also more of an adventure. Britain's most famous point-to-point is the Man-vs-Horse-vs-Mountain Bike in Wales (a mountain biker has won it twice, horses every other time). Switzerland hosts the gruelling 150km Verbier-Grimentz Race, which incorporates three 1,000m climbs along the route, which rises to 3,000m. This is reckoned to be about the toughest one-day mountain bike race in the world. In Australia there is a desert race from Sydney to Perth, which must be the world's longest mountain bike race, and once the coastal ranges have been crossed, the flattest! But in Alaska mountain bikes face the coldest challenge in the winter Iditabike test: 150km through the snow, then turn

around and go back.

Whatever the course design, much of the challenge in cross-country racing is mastering the terrain and finishing the race, both rider and bike intact.

DOWNHILL
(Fig 89)

Downhill racing was the original form of mountain bike racing, and it is also the most thrilling and dangerous. Individual riders race against the clock in this event. Many of the greatest downhill racers come from BMX or moto-cross backgrounds, and youth tends to triumph over experience. Notable exceptions do exist, such as the USA's John Tomac, who at twenty-six years old proved he was master of both cross-country and downhill racing by finishing second overall in the 1993 World Cup in both those disciplines.

The Kamikaze Downhill at Mammoth Mountain in California is the world's most famous track. Britain's David Baker holds the highest recorded maximum

Fig 89 Most downhill racers wear good protection, including padding under their outer garments.

speed for that track – 103kph, riding a bike with no suspension! 'When I got to the bottom and saw how fast I went, I thought I better give up downhill racing, it's just too dangerous', said Baker, who was twenty-four when he recorded that speed. Twenty-four is starting to get rather old for an internationally competitive downhill racer.

Downhill racing is for young riders with a thirst for adventure, but its psychology also demands a disciplined mind. It is an 'inner game' sport, that is, one that involves a lot of skill but in which the slower, analytical part of the brain must control the tactics rather than the skills. The skills are controlled by the faster, intuitive part of the brain.

To elaborate, riders use visualization techniques before the race. They visualize an image of a run down the course, mentally rehearsing moves they must make and lines to take along its full length. This gives them the knowledge they will need to negotiate the course at high speed. Controlling the bike is then a matter of letting the muscles do what they have been trained to do.

Penny Davidson, 1993 US Women's Downhill Champion, describes it thus: 'I feel what I'm doing on the bike right at that moment. I respond to the bike and make corrections with my balance to make me go faster. If the bike skids unexpectedly I stay relaxed and go with it.' Taking this approach means she uses her practised skills to stay upright and frees her mind to focus on the best line to take. This is how the inner game is won: the analytical side of the brain makes the tactical decisions, and intuition (in this case practised skills which need no conscious thought) controls both speed and bike handling. Downhill racers interested in more information about inner game theory should read Tim Gallwey's book.

HILLCLIMB

Since 1990 this event has progressively lost prestige. Although popular amongst North American and British riders, continental Europeans have not taken to it. Run either as an individual time trial or as a mass start event, the hillclimb has been described as 'pure pain' by Britain's uphill expert, Tim Gould. It is a

Fig 90   Britain's Deb Murrell grimaces on a long uphill haul.

severe test of skills and fitness best suited to riders with an excellent power-to-weight ratio.

DUAL SLALOM

A very popular event, the dual slalom is dominated by riders from a BMX background. Events normally take a knockout format, with two riders racing on parallel courses simultaneously. Both watching and competing in these events is wildly exciting. Riders do all they can to milk extra speed from their bikes, and many overdo it, resulting in an event of thrills and spills. It is great fun and – like downhill racing – is dependent on good psychological skills.

TRIALS

Also named 'trialsin', this is the most contemplative form of mountain bike competition. It is also just about the most friendly, as riders are very open with each other discussing the merits of different lines through a section and are always appreciative of those who do best.

The idea of observed trials came from motor cycle sport. Competitors ride through a series of short, marked-out, sections of terrain where it is difficult not to touch a foot or even to get off and walk. The object is not speed, but good balance. Every time a rider has to balance on something other than the bike (putting a foot down, for example), at least one point is added. The winner is the one with least points after completing all sections.

ENDURO

Enduro is also an event adapted from motor cycle competition. It presents the most complete set of challenges of all mountain bike events. It is scored like trials – the fewer points accumulated on the scorecard, the better. Paced by a theoretical optimum time to complete each stage, the rider has to go through a series of challenges. These challenges cover a broad range of skills and riders incur penalty points for mistakes. Challenge sections have both overt and covert assessment, and they typically include map reading, highway code, mountain bike code, trials skills, speed tests, and general riding skills.

PATH-FINDING EVENTS

This advanced form of mountain bike competition was inspired by the sport of orienteering. It involves spending a night out in a tent and carrying all the necessary equipment in a backpack (panniers are an unacceptable burden for rough-terrain riding). Riders travel in teams of two, which are issued at the start with a map detailing checkpoints to be visited over the weekend. Points are awarded at these checkpoints. The team with most points at the end of the weekend wins.

Determining a route is complicated because some checkpoints carry more points than others. Predictably enough, the high-scoring checkpoints can be hard to find or are at far-flung locations on the map. Riders must be able to make rapid decisions based on their assessment of how long it takes to cover different types of terrain and their own ability to keep to a schedule. Contrary to the case with downhill, in path-finding events, experience often beats youth.

Sam Cook and Colin Davidson, 1993 winners of Britain's International Polaris Challenge, list ten keys to their success.

1. Be compatible with your partner. Always stay together, help each other. If one of us is suffering the other waits for him. Ride the same gears and at the same pace.
2. The night before the event, when you get your grid references, mark your map up – don't do it on the day! We always highlight every track between the points, and then we try to work out distances and ride time between points. Then we cover the map with plastic to stop it smudging.

3. One of us always has a computer on his bike. We leave it running for the time and reset the distances after each checkpoint. This helps tremendously with time judgement.
4. Whenever possible, we use light-weight disposable kit: foil containers, plastic bages, etc. The more you can ditch after use, the lighter your load. (Obviously this should be done without leaving litter in the countryside.)
5. Each of you should have specific tasks, which should be worked out beforehand. That way you're more efficient. For instance, Sam does the tent and cooking, and Colin deals with the bikes.
6. It's always best to carry your kit in a rucksack. It's a lot easier to lift your bike over gates or push it across bogs if it's unencumbered by kit.
7. Either buy or make yourself a bar-mounted map board. It will save you a lot of time, as you can read it while on the move.
8. We eat all the time, usually complex carbohydrate fluid, like Leppin sachets. Whether you're hungry or not, in an event like this, you have to eat continually and efficiently.
9. When you get your points score sheet just after you start, always take your time working out your route. Never panic and rush things. You've got five hours or so on the bike; two minutes shaved off your marking-up time could ruin the whole event.
10. Drink all the time. We only carry one bottle each, but whenever we see a stream, we top them up. In Scotland the water is usually safe to drink.

Riders should check locally about the purity of the water in the area where an event is to be held. Untreated water across the world is becoming less and less safe to drink.

HOW TO FIND AN EVENT AND WHAT TO TAKE

Regular reading of the cycling magazines is the most effective way of finding out about mountain bike events in any given area. Magazines normally sub-divide events into different types and then categorize them by area.

If you can't make a weekend of it, at least make a day of a mountain bike event. What strikes many newcomers to mountain bike events is the active off-bike social life. Mountain bikers are a friendly lot, so why not take the necessary provisions to stay around and enjoy the atmosphere.

Riders who arrive at the race with their bike in race-ready condition then have far more time to spend examining the course, watching other races and enjoying the social scene. Repairs that are left until arrival at the race site have an unfortunate habit of turning into major operations, which does nothing for your peace of mind.

So much time can be saved while racing if you have already decided how to tackle certain sections, that it is almost essential to conduct a detailed course examination before your race. Ideally this would be the day before the race. You can often learn a lot from other riders. Wear some clothes other than your race kit for checking the course. If it's wet, you'll see a lot of sense in this.

Races can be over-subscribed. For this reason, as well as the very good reason of avoiding lengthy queues, it is

Race Requirements
1. Choice of tyres for wet and dry conditions
2. Spare wheel (if owned)
3. A spare inner tube
4. Spare brake and gear cables
5. Spare chain
6. Full tool set (*see* chapter 9)
7. Safety pins and tag ties for race number
8. Pocket toolkit:
    inner tube
    puncture kit
    tyre levers
    allen keys and spanners for
        brakes, gears, headstem
9. Packing tape. It has over a thousand uses
10. Race food (fresh bananas are hard to beat)
11. First-aid kit (be sure to include cotton swabs, and antiseptic to clean and paint grazes)
12. Towel and flannel (they will both get very dirty)
13. Warm tracksuit and comfy shoes for afterwards
14. Food and plenty of water for afterwards (make a picnic perhaps: pasta or potato salad, or creamed rice, are all ideal as post-race food)
15. Wellington boots and umbrella (if wet)
16. Sunhat and sunscreen (if sunny)
17. Bucket, sponge and dishwashing brush for bike
18. Chain lube

advisable always to send in an entry at least two weeks in advance of the race.

Finally, if you have one, don't forget your racing licence!

WHAT RACING IS LIKE
(Figs 91–93)

If you have set yourself to go hard over the distance, it can be a brutal struggle to make it to the end. If you are not up with the front-runners, cross-country racing becomes a battle between rider and terrain. You'll know what I mean if you have ever confronted a steep uphill when you are hurt and feel tired and know that you have to ride it, not once but twice more before the end of the race. With all the pain and suffering that can accompany a tough cross-country event, it is an easy target for the critics, but for those who enjoy it, the sport is unsurpassed.

I would like to offer a word to teenage mountain bike racers at this point. Pro riders sometimes live like monks in their search for maximum physical condition. This is fine for a rider in his mid-twenties, but most pros, you will find, had a fairly active social scene going when they were teenagers. Mountain bike star, Tim Gould, writing in a magazine column, once advised keen teenage mountain bike racers to 'go out to the pub, have girlfriends, have a laugh and when you've done all that get serious about mountain bike racing'.

Fig 91 Tim Gould: one of mountain bike racing's legends.

Fig 92 Mountain biking is not all blood, sweat and tears.

Fig 93   Some riders encourage the lighter side of racing.

Mental toughness is an important component of mountain bike racing. Even seasoned campaigners report wanting to climb off and rest for a bit during races. This talk of pain and anguish is not intended to put you off; it is simply to let you know that you are not alone in your suffering. The sport may be painful at times, but if the pain was not outweighed by an even greater sense of enjoyment, the competitive side of the sport would not have such a vast worldwide following.

SPECIFIC SKILLS

Cross-Country
(Figs 94–102)

The technical skills in cross-country racing are all about flowing over the terrain: keeping a smooth rhythm, using weight shifts to carry the rider over obstacles rather than jar against them, and never slowing to a stop.

Many courses involve obstacles or hills that cannot be ridden. As you get to know your limits, you will become more skilled at anticipating whether or not to ride difficult sections. If you choose to dismount, there is a certain method to use which loses little momentum.

Fig 94   Fording a wet ditch at speed. Expert bike handler Carl Sturgeon rises briefly from the seat to absorb the shock better. Note his finger position on the brakes. He is covering them in case they are needed.

THE RACING DISMOUNT

Fig 95   The racing dismount: the rider leans forward, putting more weight on his hands and swings his right leg over the seat.

Fig 96   His right leg passes in between his left leg, which remains on the pedal, and the bike frame. He is about to step onto his right foot, turning his left foot out of the pedal simultaneously.

Fig 99   Stepping off the left foot, the right leg is swung clear of the rear wheel. The rider's eyes are incorrectly focused. He should be looking ahead. There is no need to look for the pedals at this point; the rider should already have made a mental note of the pedal position.

Fig 100   The rider has to make sure to leap high enough to clear the seat, but too high and the landing will surely be painful.

Fig 97 Approaching the obstacle the rider raises the bike, while still on the run.

Fig 98 The rider does a running jump over the obstacle, and the bike is immediately replaced on the ground.

Fig 101 The rider's feet find the pedals almost immediately.

Fig 102 Off again.

On all but the smoothest of tracks, you are constantly making small weight shifts. Where possible, it is best to remain seated, but as the bumps get big you should stand on the pedals. In both positions your body moves back or forwards on the bike to cope with the ups and downs.

That may all sound rather obvious, but watch riders like Juli Furtado, David Baker, Thomas Frischknecht, or Ned Overend; they give the impression of flowing over the terrain. This is achieved by frequently moving back, lifting the handlebars and hopping the back wheel over obstacles. Not only does this reduce shock-induced fatigue, it also helps reduce speed loss. In mountain bike racing, time is gained by staying alert and constantly milking the terrain for all the speed it can offer, not by fighting against it hoping that brute strength will prevail. Finesse is just as important as strength in cross-country racing.

Downhill
(Figs 103–105)

Examine the downhill course, find the fastest lines through the obstacles and corners, then memorize the course. A good cornering line is particularly important. According to two-time British Downhill Champion, Jason McRoy, 'There's no hard and fast rule to follow when looking for a fast line on a turn … On wide, sweeping turns you'll find that starting wide and following a wide line all the way around will be the most effective technique, but you need to experiment until you're comfortable with your approach'.

Fig 103   The fastest line is frequently out of the loose stuff.

Memorization and anticipation are essential skills for downhilling. If you know what's coming, you will be able to react in time to control each obstacle with a minimum loss of speed. Therefore, you should create a mental picture of the entire course, which you rehearse several times in your mind, thinking about your gear selection, braking, slides, jumps, landings, pedalling: everything.

When performing mental rehearsal, you should take special care to think positively about the ride. You should think about the perfect ride, accounting for all the entries and exits to corners and difficult sections. If anything goes wrong in this mental rehearsal, you should go back to the start and begin again. You will then have a feeling that you have cracked the course. This form of mental rehearsal has become

Fig 104   DCD chain tensioner: a must for downhillers.

standard in many sports now. A good comparison is downhill ski racing.

Reading the course is another important cognitive skill. Many technically gifted riders come unstuck because they take risks in the wrong places. In a fundamentally risky sport, it is critical to learn where not to take risks.

Yet another important skill is being fully acquainted with a sliding bike. Locking the wheels is best avoided where possible, as it loses time, but often the bike does drift a little. Two-wheel drifting around corners is common, although not always considered by downhill racers to be good form, and you should know how to handle it when it happens.

It is not always enough for downhill racers to use oversize chain rings (60-tooth rings are common for fast courses); they still bounce off unless restraining devices are used. Riders use up to three devices to keep chains from unshipping themselves. The photograph shows a DCD chain tensioner, one of the few commercially available devices to keep chains aboard. Another common device commonly used by riders, which they make themselves, is mounted where the front derailleur would go, and it guides the chain onto the chain ring.

A low position on the bike increases speed. The faster you travel, the more aerodynamics comes into play. You should be careful, however, not to chip your teeth on the handlebars when in the aerodynamic tuck.

You should use the brakes as little as possible. This may sound odd, but control is actually easier when the brakes aren't engaged. The idea is to wash off speed with the brakes before entering an area of technical difficulty. If you know what's coming, you will be able to start applying the brakes sufficiently far in advance that speed and rhythm interruption are minimized.

Many top downhillers dangle the inside leg through a corner. They do this to help control the bike if it slides out. It also lowers their centre of gravity.

Try not to jump. As in downhill ski racing, flying will slow you down. Many riders will pre-jump, to land just after the lip which would otherwise have launched them much further. It takes some time to learn the correct timing for this manoeuvre, as it is off-putting to land the rear wheel on the crest of the hill.

knee
turned
in

Fig 105   Dangling a leg is useful if correctly performed, but it takes some practice to learn this technique.

7

Fitness for Health and Racing

Loughborough University's professor of Sports Science once humorously remarked during a lecture, 'the holy trinity of physical training is intensity, duration and frequency'. Wittiness aside, this principle shapes all sports training; by varying the ratios of these three factors we can train for every purpose and change our level of physical condition.

The key to effective training – for any purpose – lies in the rider achieving suitable ratios for the type of riding mostly performed, be it recreational or sporting. This means finding the right balance between high-intensity and low-intensity training and getting sufficient rest periods in between sessions.

EAT AND BIKE FOR A HEALTHIER LIFE

The best way to get fit for mountain biking is to get out on the trails and ride. Unlike sports like skiing, where participants go out and exercise in an unfamiliar way for whole days at a time, mountain biking starts at the home of the rider, and can be taken at first in very small doses. Therefore, pre-conditioning of the appropriate muscle groups is not necessary.

If general good health is your goal, dietary considerations are almost as important as the exercise. Nutritional needs change when you start a regular programme of exercise. Simply fuelling your body for normal activity requires intake ratios of about 15 per cent protein, 30 per cent fat and 55 per cent carbohydrate. At the other end of the scale, endurance athletes – and mountain biking is primarily an endurance sport – have to eat a ratio of around 15 per cent protein, 10 per cent fat and 75 per cent carbohydrate. Good sources of protein are white and red meats, pulses, fish and eggs. If using oil in cooking, olive oil is a better form than most. Carbohydrates are readily available in potatoes, pasta, rice and bread (preferably wholemeal).

In addition to those figures, a broad spectrum of vitamins and minerals is essential. These are better consumed in the form of fruit and vegetables (which also provide essential fibre) than in tablet form. The body can forget how to extract vitamins and minerals from regular food when tablets provide such a readily available source.

Readers of this section are not expected to embark on rides of more than two hours' duration, certainly not before having done several weeks' build-up. Also, it is expected that the intensity will be low to moderate – overdoing it can be more risky than not doing it at all. Therefore, a 5 to 10 per cent increase in

(a) Shoulder stretch

(b) Shoulder stretch

(c) Shoulder stretch

(d) Forearm and wrist stretch

(e) Backstretch

(f) Back stretch

(g) Back and leg stretch

(h) Groin and hip stretch

(i) Quadriceps

(j) Achilles stretch

(k) Groin stretch

(l) Hip stretch

(m) Hamstring stretch

(n) Calf stretch

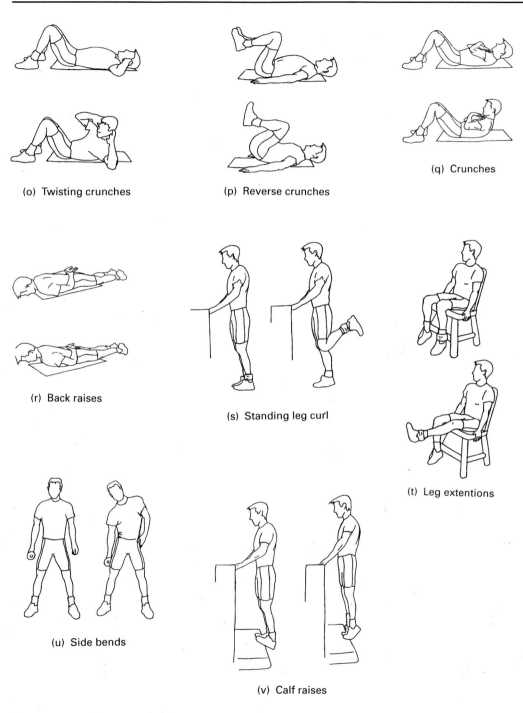

(o) Twisting crunches

(p) Reverse crunches

(q) Crunches

(r) Back raises

(s) Standing leg curl

(t) Leg extentions

(u) Side bends

(v) Calf raises

Figs 106 (a–v) Exercises for fitness.

(a) Leg lunges

(b) Press ups

(c) Rhomboid raises

(d) Tricep dips

(e) One-arm rows

Figs 107 (a–e) Further fitness exercises.

the ratio of carbohydrate in the diet, and a corresponding decrease of fat intake should take care of the changing energy demand accompanying taking up mountain biking. By all means eat more, but make it more bread, pasta, potatoes and fruit juice.

Starting regular exercise without changing your current diet could lead to feelings of fatigue and lethargy and decrease in work performance. If this happens, don't immediately blame the exercise; there could be a variety of ways to solve the problem. In any case young and mature adults should talk

with their doctor about things like diet and organ function if taking up mountain biking after a sedentary lifestyle.

The key is to ease into exercise. There is no such thing as getting fit quickly. Mountain biking is great fun, and you might be tempted to stay out too long or go out too frequently at first, but the likely result of this is excessive fatigue and possibly a crash following that. It is far better to stay hungry for that weekend mountain bike ride, just going out one morning a week for the first four to six weeks.

The other thing to be considered is

that regular exercise involves a lifestyle change. Even if that exercise involves riding into work, common sense dictates that such change should be eased in gradually. The general programme described here does not include riding to work, which involves too many variables in terrain and distance to account for. However, daily exercise – such as riding to work – is commonly regarded by health experts as being one of the most reliable paths to good health.

Start with weekly rides of between 30 and 120 minutes' duration, being careful to keep the effort at a low intensity. Along with exercise should come a muscle stretching programme. Stretching helps prepare you for exercise and also aids recovery. It is best to stretch when the blood and muscles have warmed. This can mean stepping off the bike after ten minutes' riding, stretching for ten minutes, then continuing. You should wear warm clothing covering the full limbs when the air temperature is under 15 degrees Celsius. Stretching at the end of a ride helps clear the muscles of waste products which have built up during exercise.

After four to six weeks, you could choose to increase to two such rides each week, including one mid-week in the early morning or after work. For many people, two rides a week will be sufficient exercise, especially if riding to work as well. Perhaps you will choose to do some off-bike conditioning to supplement the riding.

If you want more exercise than the two prescribed weekly rides, there are several options. The best of these is to increase the frequency and reduce the duration of the rides, perhaps moving up to four rides of one hour each week.

However, this can be difficult to fit in with all the other things one has to do, so it becomes a matter of getting the most out of the available riding time. Five hours' recreational cycling a week is a good figure for the average adult after some three months' regular riding, but if this can only be got in two sessions, it is not likely to carry as much of a health benefit as it would spread out over four or more sessions.

High-intensity exercise will lead to gains in physical condition, but medical experts do not rate this as the most beneficial option health-wise. It is seen as placing a heavy strain on various of the body's systems. Exercising at an intensity you judge to be between moderate and brisk strikes a happy medium that will not strain your body unduly. Some who take up mountain biking for health reasons find within themselves a latent passion for a hard work-out on the bike. These people might like to consider racing, where the majority of riders are there not to win, but just for the excitement and fun of a good hard ride in the company of like-minded individuals.

GENERAL TRAINING POINTS
Cross-Country

The heaviest energy demand in cross-country mountain bike racing is placed on the aerobic endurance system, but anaerobic endurance and explosive bursts are also necessary, as was explained in the discussion of hill-climbing skills (such places are short stretches which are very steep, where a five-second burst of work will save you from having to dismount). Therefore, for

	Aerobic System	Lactate System	Phosphate Battery
Energy Supply	aerobic	anaerobic	anaerobic
Energy Source	combining fat or carbohydrate with oxygen	glycogen	ATP and creatine phosphate (PCr)
Duration	many hours	2–3 min	10–15 sec
Mountain Bike Racing Use	most of the time	making a break or on a climb	short, very steep climbs; sprinting to the line

Table 2   Energy Sources.
The body has three main energy sources: (1) Aerobic system, (2) Lactic system, (3) Phosphate battery. In everyday activity, the body uses these systems in combination.

cross-country racing the training programme will focus on aerobic endurance, but attention should also be paid to the anaerobic energy production systems.

Quality training is an often misused term. What it really means is dedicating one training session to one energy system. This way you can pin-point areas for development. A course that is good fun to ride may not be so good for training purposes. For example, it may allow too much or too little rest in between sets of high intensity riding; or it may prevent a constant heart rate where steady state training is the object. Cross-country racing puts the training focus on the legs and cardio-vascular system. Some regular upper-body training is recommended, but mainly with low weight and high repetitions (twenty-five and up). Because of the amount of climbing in a cross-country race, power output to body weight is a crucial ratio in determining how good a rider's body is for this event. As muscle is the heaviest of all body tissue, the rider is not encouraged to develop large, explosively strong muscles.

Downhill

The downhill race requires maximum pedalling effort and upper-body control all the way. The famous all-rounder, John Tomac, commented after a World Cup downhill race at Mont-Sainte-Anne, Canada, '192 (beats per minute), that's the highest heart rate I have recorded all season'. In that rate Tomac had achieved a higher intensity of work than he had done in any of the cross-country races that season.

Downhillers need to train their muscles to prolong functionality in a lactate-rich environment. Near-maximum heart rates during exercise normally coincide with measurably high concentrations of lactic acid (lactate). Special training is required to build a tolerance to lactate, as this acidic by-product of high-intensity exercise is widely regarded to cause muscle dysfunction, which leads to a loss of coordination and increases the risk of error, not to mention a decrease in pedalling force and grip on the handlebars.

Downhill racers can expect to focus on lactate tolerance and sprint training, but a good endurance base is also important for this type of racing. Furthermore, downhill racers will benefit more from extra upper- and lower-body muscle bulk than cross-country racers do.

Extra upper-body strength can be helpful in controlling the bike on rough terrain. In downhill racing, the power to body weight ratio is not as important as the absolute power output. Good bike handling skills and mental discipline are as important as physiology to the downhill racer.

Low-intensity, high-intensity and sprint work are all fuelled by different energy systems. The following table provides a brief guide to the energy systems and their respective contributions to the mountain biking effort.

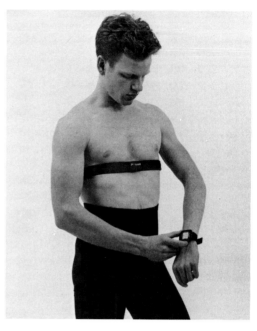

Fig 108 Heart rate monitors represent a major advance in training effectiveness but only when used in conjunction with a structured training programme.

TRAINING CONCEPTS

For serious racers, I recommend using a heart rate monitor. If correctly used, this can greatly increase the accuracy of training and therefore be far more significant to your race performance than any piece of lightweight componentry.

Using a heart rate monitor enables you to see which of the energy systems is predominantly being used. Detailed information about using heart rate monitors can be found in books, but the one thing that is essential to know is how to calculate percentages of the heart rate range. For example, we use the random figure of 70 per cent. Seventy per cent of the heart rate (HR) range is determined thus:

93

(HRmax–HRmin) x 70 per cent + HRmin = 70 per cent HR range. (Heart rate percentages given in this chapter are calculated using this formula.)

One of the most important concepts is that of progressive overload and recovery. Overloading the body causes it some damage. Therefore, it adjusts itself so that next time the same amount of overload will cause it less damage.

This change doesn't take place instantly, which is why a period of recovery is important after hard training sessions. Changes within the muscles and the cardio-vascular system take place during the period of recovery. It can take up to forty-eight hours to recover from anaerobic training sessions. During this recovery period, it is unwise to tax the anaerobic systems. If the muscle is put under repeated overload without adequate periods of recovery intervening, the result is a progressive decline. I have seen this happen on many occasions. It's very easy to overtrain and the result is always the same: poor performance.

Recovery is aided by taking carbo-hydrates immediately after the race, say a litre bottle of carbohydrate solution mixed to a 25 per cent concentration. The other big influence in recovery is drinking water, but it is less important in recovery than during exercise.

Deflection Point

As exercise intensity gets harder and harder, there is a point at which blood lactate starts to accumulate at a much faster rate than previously.

More Tea, Vicar?

As a junior, I rode a fifty-mile road race without taking a water bottle. 'Save weight', I cunningly thought to myself. During that race I felt thirsty and regretted my mistake in not carrying water. Late in the race, I was unable to go with a key move that would have put me on the podium. Had I not been so dehydrated, I expect I would have felt good enough to make that extra effort.

Some junior riders now are just as 'cunning' as I was then. Some tell me they train without water to condition themselves to race without water. This makes no sense. At an ambient tem-perature of 10 degrees Celsius an exercising body can lose one litre of water per hour. Water is needed by the body's cooling system; it also transports nutrients throughout the tissues, and it maintains an adequate blood volume. It is a common mistake to rely on feeling thirsty as the signal to drink. Thirst is in fact a distress signal sent out by an already dehydrated body. Riders must drink before they feel thirsty: 200ml every 10–15 minutes should replace what is lost during exercise.

Periods of Training

Another important concept in training is periodization. The body goes through cycles of training, starting off with very easy aerobic (endurance) training, progressing ultimately to lactate and PCr training. The total time for this pro-gression should be about five to six months, and the endurance period should start about a month after the racing season has ended.

The reason for progressing through a series of training periods is that working at high intensity the muscle has to function in an environment of high acidity. This environment is damaging to the muscle, and so it is a matter of preparing the muscle in order to limit the damage. Through a progressive build-up, the muscle is slowly introduced to increasing acid levels and therefore is better able to function in, and recover from, high acidity.

Keeping a base line of endurance training throughout the periods of build-up to the season, you will then go through the following phases: extensive endurance, intensive endurance, explosive power, lactate tolerance, racing season, and recuperation.

What the Sessions Involve

The sessions described below are given code names that correspond to those used in the tables that follow.

EXTENSIVE ENDURANCE
Session codes: LIE (Low-Intensity Endurance); HIE (High Intensity Endurance).

Endurance riding is performed at a constant heart rate, called steady-state training. In practice this would mean holding back up hills and working harder on the descents in order to keep the heart rate constant. Flat roads are best for endurance training. Endurance training can be high- or low-intensity. It takes a lot of courage and motivation to complete a high-intensity extensive endurance session effectively, but the advantage is that it can be performed in a group.

INTENSIVE ENDURANCE
Session code: AP (Aerobic Power).

This involves endurance intervals, which should improve the stroke volume (the quantity of blood your heart puts out with each beat). These sessions are best performed alone, but can still be effective with a training partner, although riding at your own pace. The sessions can be done on or off road, and cross-country racers should perform them sitting in the seat, pedalling at 60rpm, going up a hill. If done off road, an added benefit is gained in riding skill, provided different hills are used for the sessions.

Downhillers can also perform this training on or off road. Like cross-country racers, it should be done seated and at about 60rpm. Downhill, flat terrain or turbo trainers should be used.

EXPLOSIVE POWER
Session code: PCr (Phospho-creatine).

This is simply to develop explosive power over a short distance. Accordingly, the training builds stronger muscles and makes them able to recruit more muscle fibres for the effort.

For cross-country racers, it is very useful for short, steep climbs and getting up very short, very steep patches on long climbs without having to dismount. Such terrain should therefore be used for this training.

Downhillers may find that some events are a series of flat-out sprints separated by short technical stretches. Downhillers should perform PCr training on flat and downhill terrain.

LACTATE TOLERANCE
Session code: LT (Lactate Tolerance).

These sessions are intended to familiarize the muscle with what it will probably experience during a race: a build-up of lactic acid. The training develops the muscles' systems for removing and reprocessing this by-product of anaerobic exercise. LT training is said to cause damage to the aerobic systems, so it should not be a frequent component of your training programme. The training is performed on road, off road, or if necessary on a turbo trainer. Downhillers are recommended to use big gears on flat ground, whereas cross-country riders could benefit more from smaller gears on uphills.

RECOVERY RIDING
Session code: REC (Recovery).

This is just as important as any other training in the programme. Easy riding increases blood flow through muscles, bringing rich oxygen and nutrient supplies when they may be most needed, without fatiguing the muscle. This training can be performed on or off road on a flat circuit. If going off road, it is better to stick to relatively smooth trails. Provided the intensity remains light, some off-road skills may be practised on recovery rides.

Cross-country and downhill racers can use all of these training sessions. The difference comes in the balance of the different types of training session used. Broad guide lines on finding the correct balance are given in the following tables.

Session Code	Intensity	Duration of Each Repetition	Volume (Total of Repetitions And Sets)	Rest	Mode	Type
PCr	maximum effort	10–15 sec	set up to 1 min (total up to 6 min)	2–3 min between reps 5–6 min between sets	off road	interval
LT	near-maximum (at least 90% effort)	1–2 min	Total of reps (10–20 min)	3-4 min between reps	on or off road	interval
AP	hard (80–85%)	4–6 min	Total of reps (40–60 min)	3-4 min between reps	on or off road	interval
HIE	hard (80–85%) (maximum sustainable)	30–90 min	60–90 min	none or 15 min	on road	steady state
LIE	moderate to brisk (60–70 %)	90–180 min	90–180 min	none	on road	steady state
REC	easy (<60 %)	90–180 min	90–180 min	if desired	on or off road	steady state

Notes:

1. Warm up with stretching for each session.

2. Where a rider has scheduled four / five days training each week, rest days and REC rides should be flexible. If the rider feels tired in the morning a rest day or REC ride should be done that day. If tiredness continues over several days, training volume should be reduced immediately.

3. All interval times are for a rolling start.

4. All rest periods during interval training sessions should be easy pedalling.

5. If combining two types of training in one session (e.g. PCr and AP) always do the highest intensity first.

Table 3 The Range of Training Sessions

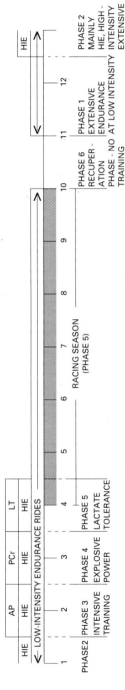

Month of year and relevant fitness phase

N.B.
1. REC rides should follow race days and particularly tough training days.

2. Use the concept of progression when entering a new phase. Start well below the figures stated in Table 3, and build up to them over the four week period.

3. During the racing season one LT session per week is enough. Pre-season two LT sessions per week is the maximum.

4. During the race season, the rider sets performance targets then builds up and tapers towards them. If not racing one weekend, try to put in a hard off-road ride instead. The base line mixture of LIE, HIE and REC training remains, with the occasional addition of AP and PCr and LT training.

Table 4 Suggested Guidelines for Annual Mountain Bike Training Programme

Sample Training Week in Phase 4 of Training year

		1 hr				
2x30 min		LIE		1 hr		
HIE	2 hr	1 hr	45 min	PCr	1 hr	rest day
1 hr	LIE	HIE	REC		HIE	
PCr						

| Sun | Mon | Tue | Wed | Thur | Fri | Sat |

Total 8 hr 45 min
22 % = PCr (N.B. Of this time only a fraction is spent in high-intensity exercise. 60 min is duration of the entire session.)
34 % = HIE 34 % = LIE 9 % = REC

Sample Training Week in Phase 5 (out of Race Season)

1 hr LT		90 min	1 hr LT		2 hr	
1 hr REC		HIE		45 min	LIE	rest day
	1 hr REC			REC		

| Sun | Mon | Tue | Wed | Thur | Fri | Sat |

Total 8 hr 15 min
24 % = LT (N.B.Less than 30% of this time is spent in LT exercise itself.)
18 % = HIE 24 % = LIE 33 % = REC

N.B. This training device is for an already-fit adult racer. Novices and teenagers should halve the sample workloads.

Table 5 Cross Country Training

Downhill riders can combine the skills component with these exercises where they consider it safe to do so, but generally the skills aspect should be trained in addition to the sample schedules.

PREPARING FOR IMPORTANT RACES

After years of racing, you will start to get a feel for how your body works. The well-informed athlete is best equipped to maximize his potential. From experience I know that each year I reach a physical peak around mid-August. This happens regardless of the training I am doing. If you can identify such a pattern in your fitness levels, it can be a good morale booster to train around this and target a specific race. The race then becomes one to look forward to, even if it is not a championship event.

Good form can also be nurtured for one or two important races each year by the use of training build-up, followed by a brief taper period. You will perform fine tuning to race-season fitness by training hard with longer sessions for a few weeks, then over two weeks reduce training duration and increase intensity and rest.

During the week of the big race, carbohydrate stores should be increased in preparation for the race. This can be done in the four days leading up to the race by eating more carbohydrates – preferably in complex form (potatoes, pasta, rice, etc.)

Sample Training Week in Phase 3

Sun	Mon	Tue	Wed	Thu	Fri	Sat
PCr 30 min AP 60 min	1 hr REC	2x30 min HIE	1 hr REC	1 hr AP 1hr REC	30 min AP 30 min HIE	rest

Total 7hr 30 min
7 % = PCr   (N.B. Mixing of sessions during
33% = AP   weeks ending and starting
20% = HIE   phases is an option.)
40% = REC

Sample Training Week in Phase 4

Sun	Mon	Tue	Wed	Thu	Fri	Sat
PCr 1 hr	1 hr LIE 30 min HIE	1 hr REC	1 hr PCr 2x30 min HIE	1 hr REC	1 hr PCr	rest

Total 7hr 30 min
40% = PCr   (N.B. Only a small fraction of
20% = HIE   this time is spent in high-intensity
13% = LIE   exercise itself.)
27% = REC

Sample Training Week in Phase 5

Sun	Mon	Tue	Wed	Thu	Fri	Sat
1 hr LT	1 hr REC	2x30 min HIE 30 min PCr	1 hr REC	1 hr LT 2x15 min HIE	rest	rest

Total 6hr
33% = LT
8% = PCr
25% = HIE
33% = REC

N.B. This training advice is for an already-fit adult athlete. Novices and teenagers should halve the sample workloads.

Table 6 Downhill Training

Cross-Country

In this period, training will be reduced to a complete rest with four days to go until the event. Ride an abbreviated HIE session (25 per cent less volume than the previous HIE ride) two clear days before the event. One clear day before the event, do either an abbreviated AP session or an abbreviated PCr (50 per cent of the previous volume) – depending on what you're more comfortable with.

On race day, finish eating (if possible) three hours before the event, and then start drinking a carbohydrate drink (7 per cent solution) 5 minutes before the race begins. The warm-up should start 30 minutes before competition. Get the body warm, stretch for 10 minutes, then ride for 15 minutes, building up to the last 5, which are ridden at HIE pace. Do four 10-second sprints, with 45 seconds for recovery in between each. Follow this with a 5-minute brisk-paced ride, and turn up at the start line as soon before the gun goes as possible.

Downhill

The emphasis on downhill is far less

99

clear cut. The psychological element of the sport can override physical condition. Three full days before the race, you should take a rest. With two full days to go, you should do an abbreviated session of AP training (25 per cent less than the previous AP session). The day before the race, you can sharpen speed with a PCr session. This should also be abbreviated (25 per cent less than the previous PCr session) and performed in the morning. The remainder of the day should be devoted to practising on the course.

On race day, try not to eat within three hours of the event. Start warming up 30 minutes before the race, even if it is only a 2-minute race. In this warm-up, after 5 minutes of exercise, you should spend 10 minutes stretching. Then – if possible – get on a turbo trainer and spend 15 minutes pedalling at a fast rate, at HIE pace. This will leave you physically warm and loose to race. Some riders do mental imaging exercises while on the turbo trainer. Others prefer to perform this form of psychological preparation off the bike.

8

Equipment

This chapter provides more on general principles than on specific pieces of equipment. Equipment advance is so rapid in mountain biking that readers looking for the most up-to-date information are best served by the special-interest press.

These days the pace of equipment change seems unnecessarily fast. Component development in mountain biking equipment bespeaks an entirely different philosophy from that which for many years predominated in road cycling equipment manufacture. Manufacturers of road cycling equipment faithfully reproduced the same reliable equipment year after year, and an alteration to a product line was big news as recently as the 1970s. Spurred by the demand for high-performance products, mountain bike component manufacturers have released upgraded models on to the market every year.

Many consumers see this as a good opportunity to purchase new equipment every year in order to keep up with the latest developments. By contrast, most mountain biking experts are generally satisfied to observe the trends, only picking up on revolutionary developments, such as Shimano's SPD pedal, or major advances in fully suspended bikes. Even then, they normally don't upgrade until what they are using wears out. Good-quality mountain bikes sold

since 1989 have generally been of a very high standard. Despite this, if a bike is frequently used off road the mud and grit soon start to grind away at equipment, and it is not unusual for tyres to last only a matter of months; likewise gear cogs, derailleurs and even wheel rims. Brake blocks and cables should be replaced even more frequently.

Head Protection and Lighting
(Figs 109–110)

Two essentials are head protection and lighting. The helmet featured here is a hard-shell design, which conforms to the SNELL and ANSI standards. These are the internationally recognized marks of approval. Helmets are generally made with a polystyrene core, which absorbs impact. Some have a hard shell covering the core; others don't. The hard-shell design probably offers slightly better protection than the soft-shell design.

The lights shown here are the minimum needed for safety and functional reasons. They do not meet legal standards in some countries, but they are compact and easily carried on off-road rides. Unfortunately, many designs that do meet the legal standards are less effective than this combination.

If you get delayed out on the trail and

101

Fig 109 Even if going out for a summer afternoon's ride, it is advisable to take a lightweight lighting system.You might have to end the ride in the dark.

Fig 110 Close up of hard shell helmet, helmet-attaching light (battery pack at rear) and clip on rear light.

must ride home in the dark, this lighting system is practical for off-road use as it is not affected by vibration passed through the bicycle frame.

CLOTHING
(Figs 111–114)

Many riders regard those illustrated here as the most comfortable shorts. The stretch-lycra fabric may look flashy, but is the most functional material to use on a bicycle. Its seamless crotch design increases comfort, the close fit to the legs makes the material less abrasive when wet and it doesn't form creases. The shoulder straps are a luxurious addition, but riders who pay extra for this design seldom complain about it.

Fig 111 Bib shorts are very popular amongst riders.

Fig 112   Different summer clothing options.

Various types of clothing worn by mountain bikers are included in Fig 112: a casual kit, the serious rider's kit and a wet-weather kit. Note that all riders are wearing glasses. Eye protection is essential for safety reasons. The greatest need is for protection against airborne insects and so on. Catching one of these in the eye when on a fast descent can be disastrous. The tighter fitting shirt is more practical than the loose shirt, with its zip neck and pockets in the rear. Its synthetic fibres also pass moisture from the inside to the outside of the fabric, and it drys much faster than the cotton material of the loose shirt. However, for many riders the sporty image of the cycling shirt is off-putting. The problem of carrying essential items if not wearing a cycling shirt is overcome by wearing a good-quality hip bag, which is less comfortable than rear pockets but is a reasonable alternative.

For light rain a lightweight jacket made of breathable fabric works well. If you are exercising hard, breatheable fabrics tend to pass moisture out more slowly than it is produced, but are a lot better than non-breathable fabrics. The jacket pictured has a low rear, to protect the seat of the pants from catching spray from the rear wheel. The sleeves have elasticated cuffs to keep draughts out, and the high collar prevents cool wind from blowing in onto the chest.

All three riders are wearing gloves. These, like glasses, are essential. The main function of gloves is to prevent the palm of the hand from being grazed in a crash. The rider wearing wet-weather kit will also appreciate the warming properties of gloves.

The casual rider is wearing loose cotton shorts with a padded seat cushion insert. These are more comfortable than ordinary shorts but still not in the same league as those worn by serious riders. For around-town riding, the pockets and more conventional design of the loose shorts make them preferable for many riders.

Even in light rain it is a good thing to cover the legs. The cooling property of wind on wet legs even at low speeds has a potentially harmful effect on exercising muscles.

When it is very cold and wet, you would be well advised to take extra measures to keep warm. Wet-weather equipment should be carried on all rides into mountainous areas and on tours, even in warm climates. The photograph shows a rider wearing a fleecy headband under his helmet, Gore-Tex cycling jacket and trousers, and neoprene overshoes. Overshoes can make a big difference to morale if faced with hours of riding in the wet. In winter conditions, they are essential, as are the full-finger, thick gloves.

The range of eye protection for mountain bikers covers a wide variety of designs. Light weight is an important feature, as heavier glasses are more likely to slide down the nose. The wrap-around design has rightly gained popu-

Fig 113   Essential winter clothing.

larity, as it offers superior protection from sunburn. Glass lenses should be avoided because of the obvious risk of splintering in a crash. Damage to the eyes caused by the sun at high altitudes, and wind, can be severe enough to prevent a rider from continuing. In lesser cases the discomfort caused by sun- or wind-burned eyes can detract from an otherwise enjoyable experience. Here illustrated is a range of popular designs.

REHYDRATION
(Figs 115–116)

Rehydration is an important consider-

Fig 114 Eye protection is advised for general riding.

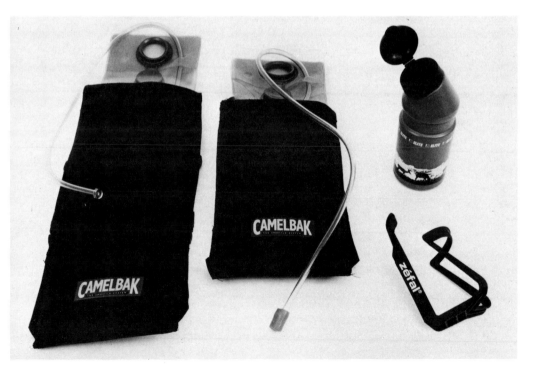

Fig 115 Camelbak water-carrying devices next to the traditional bottle-and-cage set up.

105

ation for mountain bikers. Scientists have suggested that a rider exercising at a moderate intensity should drink at least 100ml of water every 10–15 minutes. The safest way of carrying water is in a special backpack, illustrated here. A tube is clipped to the shirt, and the rider just needs to bite on a mouthpiece to receive a jet of water in the mouth. The rider is able to carry one or two litres in small- or large-size packs. The jet of water is off-putting for some riders, but most who use this system swear by it. Riders who prefer the water bottle can obtain specially reinforced cages for mountain bike use.

Fig 116 How the Camelbak is worn: note the feeding tube over the shoulder.

PUMPS
(Fig 117)

The range of tyre inflation devices illustrated here can fill the tyre with air in as little as 10 seconds (for the big track pump) and as much as 3 minutes (for the smallest pump). Track pumps cannot be carried on a bike, but with an air-pressure gauge they are very useful for setting the correct tyre pressure before setting out. The two medium-sized pumps will both fit on a bicycle. One is held in place by the frame tubes, the other by special clips purchased with the pump.

FOOTWEAR
(Figs 118–120)

Footwear is now designed with specific purposes in mind. Here is a range of suggested combinations of footwear and pedals. The shoes on the left are intended for a lot of walking and scrambling as well as biking. They are more comfortable for walking than the other two designs but will not grip the pedal as effectively. They have been matched with a set of pedals fitted with toe clips. As a minimum measure, it is strongly recommended that riders use toe clips, which prevent the foot slipping off the front of the pedal as well as increasing pedalling efficiency.

The shoes and pedals in the middle are a lightweight racing set-up. The shoes have a fairly rigid sole with an aggressive tread for good traction if running up muddy slopes. They would not be very comfortable for walking in. These shoes attach to the small pedal with the clip, which is also pictured. The

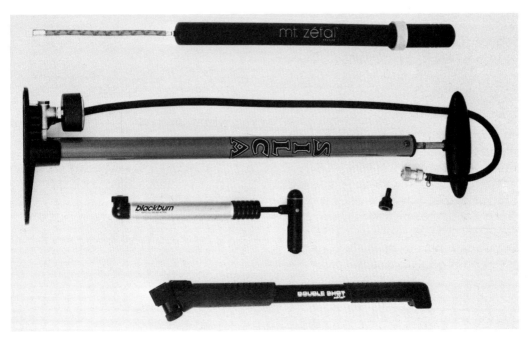

Fig 117   The range of bicycle pumps.

Fig 118   Different shoes and pedals for discerning riders.

Fig 119   The SPD pedal with platform attachment.

Fig 120   The SPD pedal.

clip is bolted to a recess in the shoe so does not affect walking. The pedal itself has clips on both sides and is very quickly snapped into by the cleated shoe. Elastomer springs clamp the cleat, and when you want to remove your foot, you simply rotate the heel outwards.

The set-up on the right is a classic general-purpose arrangement. It could be used for racing, touring or re-creational riding. The pedal is the renowned Shimano SPD, which has coil springs where the other clipless pedal has elastomers. Likewise, the cleat is recessed into the shoe and does not hinder walking.

The clipless method of shoe fastening is one of the major advances in cycling efficiency and control. Using clipless pedals you have greater control over the bike on the downhill, where steering force can be exerted through the pedals, and better efficiency on uphills and in jumps, where it is an advantage to pull up on the pedal.

The close-up views of the SPD clipless pedal show it with and without the accessory platform that is needed to convert it to use for everyday shoes. Touring riders should also use this device. The only real drawback of pedals that attach to the foot in some way is that you cannot exit the pedal instantly. In some situations, for example a very exposed track above a big drop, you may be compelled instantly to jettison the bike. This can be done if using the SPD platforms.

Fig 121 Various different approaches to handlebar extensions are available.

BAR ENDS
(Figs 121–122)

The range of hand grip options and the bio-mechanical efficiency of the flat mountain bike handlebars can be increased by using handlebar extensions, commonly called 'bar ends'. They are particularly useful for climbing. Not only do they offer an arm position that yields a more forceful synergy of the arm muscles, they also position more weight over the front wheel. The latter effect gives better steering control on steep climbs. The photographs illustrate different types of bar ends and detail how they look when mounted on the handlebars. The curved design allows extra hand grip positions over the straight designs.

Fig 122 Simple handlebar ends mounted. Some riders prefer a steeper mount, others prefer the bar ends to be mounted flatter.

109

PROTECTION
(Figs 124–127)

An English company has reacted to the strong demand in Britain for products that protect the mountain bike rider – and the bike – from the mud. Conventional mud guards are no good because they soon clog up and prevent the wheel from turning. The devices illustrated here have proved to be effective designs. The Crud Guard not only keeps mud pellets out of the back pockets but also from oozing down into the seat tube. It is mounted on rubberized blocks to prevent mounting screws from coming loose with vibration. Manufacturers of luggage-carrying systems should exam-

Fig 124   The Crud Guard.

Fig 123   The legendary Crud Catcher keeps mud spray off the face.

ine the possibilities presented by this concept.

There is also a device called the Crud Claw, which cleans mud out of the gears while the bike is in motion. This is of particular benefit to racing cyclists, but is useful to anyone who has to contend with thick mud.

Brake boosters have also been designed to meet specific needs of mountain biking. The strength of the cantilever brakes is such that when the brakes are applied hard, the frame tubes they are mounted on can be pushed apart, which has adverse effects on the braking performance. Brake boosters provide reinforcement for the tubes.

Fig 125 The Crud Claw. The teeth scrape mud out of the gear cogs while the bike is on the move.

Fig 126 Rear brake booster: improves braking performance and eliminates squeal.

Fig 127 Front brake boosters are necessary if using suspension forks, which are more susceptible than ordinary forks to being pushed apart by the strength of the cantilever brakes.

Essential Equipment
1. Helmet
2. Front and rear lights
3. A bike lock
4. Pump
5. Toolkit
6. Water bottle
7. Fingerless gloves (called 'mitts')
8. Proper cycling shorts
9. Cycling shirt with rear pockets or else hip pack to carry tools
10. Glasses with interchangeable lenses (for different light conditions)
11. Wet-weather kit

Luxury Items
1. Titanium
2. Fully suspended bike
3. The wide world of cutting-edge specialist accessories

Desirable Equipment
1. Clipless pedals (essential for the enthusiast mountain biker)
2. Crud Catcher (in muddy conditions)
3. Heart rate monitor (essential for racing cyclists)
4. Turbo trainer (essential for racing cyclists)
5. Cycle computer (essential if touring)
6. Crud Guard
7. Crud Claw
8. Front suspension
9. Brake boosters
10. Custom-built frame (if you're of unusual proportions)
11. Anti-chainsuck plates
12. Track pump

9
Maintenance

The great mountain bike racer, Mike Kloser, once said of mountain bikes, 'These bikes are so good, you can take them out, give them a thrashing in the dirt and dust, clean them up after the ride, then go out and give them the same hammering the next day ... you can keep on doing that for years'. This is only true if adequate maintenance is performed in between rides. Five or ten minutes after a ride can make all the difference.

IN-BETWEEN-RIDE CHECKS AND MAINTENANCE
(Figs 128–131)

During lengthy periods of rain it may seem futile to perform detailed cleaning operations when the bike is only going to get covered in dirt and grime next time you go out. If you don't want to take the time to perform routine cleaning and maintenance, you should consider that an unmaintained mountain bike is potentially dangerous and will be a constant source of minor problems, costing a lot more than a bike kept in clean condition. Dirt dries out cables, making the metal brittle; dirt also conceals cracks in the frame and other metal parts; finally, it is abrasive to all the moving contact surfaces, such as chains and derailleurs, and therefore makes them wear out sooner.

The first thing to do on returning from a ride is to hose or wipe down the bike: hose if it's muddy; wipe if it's dusty. If done immediately after the ride, the dirt will be easy to move. If suitable facilities for a hose are not available, a bucket and sponge will suffice. When hosing, the water jet should not be pointed directly at any bearing sets. (It is surprisingly easy to wash the grease out of bearings.)

The chain demands a lot of care and attention. Dust, water, dirt and grit are all part of the normal working environment of the chain. Unfortunately, these things are effective grinding agents, and a dirty chain will wear out not only itself, but also the cogs and the chain rings. After a certain amount of wear these have to be replaced. The main factor in the rate of wear is how frequently the transmission is cleaned.

Often the cogs need to be replaced at the same time as the chain, which is because they wear together. If the transmission is kept scrupulously clean, you can replace up to three chains before having to replace the more heavily used cogs, but it can be a problem buying rear cogs individually. Shop around a little for them.

A dirty chain is less mechanically efficient than a clean one, which is another reason why it should be cleaned after every off-road ride and realistically after every two or three rides. This

113

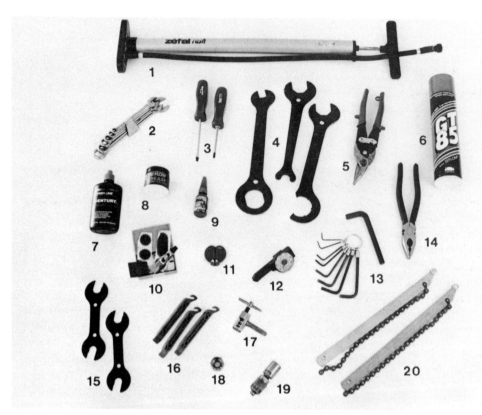

Fig 128 An average workshop toolkit: (1) track pump, (2) cone and ring spanners, (3) screw drivers, (4) headset and bottom bracket wrenches, (5) wire cutters, (6) moisture displacing spray, (7) PTFE-based lubricant, (8) PTFE bearing grease, (9) super glue, (10) puncture repair kit, (11) spoke key, (12) tyre pressure gauge, (13) metric allen key set, from 2mm up to 10mm (10mm is for removing a Shimano freewheel cassette), (14) pliers, (15)cone spanners, (16) tyre levers, (17) chain rivet extractor, (18) freewheel remover, (19) crank puller, (20) chain whips (for removing gear cogs).

simple task will be well worth it in terms of physical effort and money saved.

If using synthetic lubricants, solvents are not necessary for chain cleaning, although they are needed for the cogs. Hot water is the best chain cleaner, as it simply removes surface lube and grit without penetrating to the inside surfaces of the rollers. After being washed, the chain is best dried in an oven, a warm room or over a radiator. To maximize its effect, lubrication should then be applied while the chain is still warm. I normally wipe off the excess with a rag to make the chain less attractive to dirt and grit.

Various chain bathing devices exist, such as the one pictured here, but a stiff paintbrush will suffice. It's far easier to clean the chain on the bike than to remove it and almost as effective, but only if meticulous attention is paid to

114

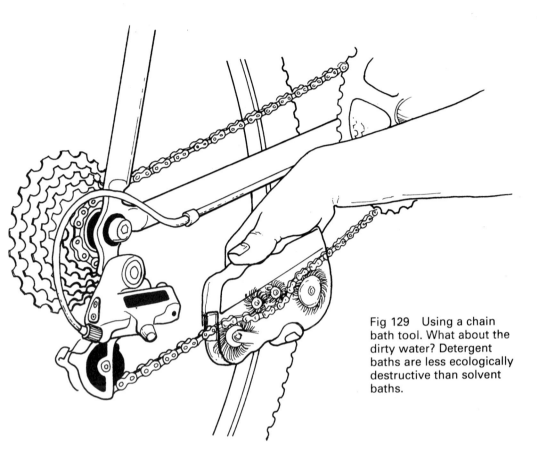

Fig 129 Using a chain bath tool. What about the dirty water? Detergent baths are less ecologically destructive than solvent baths.

getting the brush into every nook and cranny. Drying is also an important consideration. If a solvent is used it is not so critical as solvents will evaporate fairly quickly, but if water is used, then drying takes more energy. Of course, lubricants should not be applied over water as this greatly reduces their effect. If you use oil as a chain lube, then kerosene or diesel fuel make good cleaners. Petrol penetrates too deep into the rollers.

Next comes lubrication. The chain should be lubed after each ride. This is most effectively done by holding the can of lube in one place and running the chain quickly by it. I normally lube the chain as it bends over the rear cogs and then from the other side of the rollers just after it exits from the jockey wheels on the rear derailleur. A light application is sufficient. The bike should not be ridden again that day so that the lube can fully penetrate.

Different conditions call for different sorts of lube. In winter I use a heavy, mountain bike wax-based lube, which will not get washed off by ground water. The trouble is that heavy lube picks up a lot more grime than light lube. The heavy lube is also more difficult to clean off than light lube, so in winter I rarely

115

clean the chain more than twice a week, if riding regularly. If the chain looks nice and lubed, I don't always reapply lube after each ride.

For dry riding in summer I use a light, PTFE-based lube and wipe off the excess with a rag, then clean and relube the chain after every ride. If there is likely to be water on the ground, I go back to the heavy lube, which I also use if in doubt. Dry chains snap too easily. I tend to avoid oil as it picks up grime and grit, and it does not mix with synthetic lubricants.

Sometimes chains develop stiff links. Normally just bending the chain link plates sideways around the stiff pivot solves the problem.

When cleaning your bike, it is worth checking for things like dried-out or frayed cables. Frayed cables can pull through or snap when the brake lever is pulled hard. It is not uncommon for brake cables to start deteriorating just above the fastening clamp on the brake cantilever. As soon as one strand snaps, it is time to replace the cable.

CHECKING THE FRAME FOR CRASH DAMAGE
(Fig 132)

Fig 130 Stiff links aren't always this obvious, but can normally be spotted going through the rear gears.

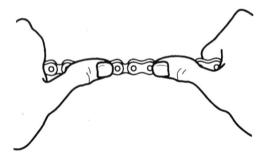

Fig 131 Manipulation with the thumbs normally fixes stiff links.

Relative to other sports, mountain biking probably carries a low risk of injuries more severe than minor abrasions, but by regularly monitoring equipment you can do a lot to make the sport even safer.

It seldom does, but the last thing you want to happen is for the front end of the bike to fold up when hopping a drainage trench on a fast descent. Impact on the front end of the bike from riding ditches and gutters, hopping, jumping, crashing, and general riding can lead to cracks appearing in the tubes where stress is greatest. Thus, you should be alert to this possible danger and try to spot any problems before they cause an accident. the front section of the main tube and top tube, just by their junctions with the head tube are the most critical places to check. Fatigue cracks are rare, but they are well worth looking for.

Checking the frame for cracks is an

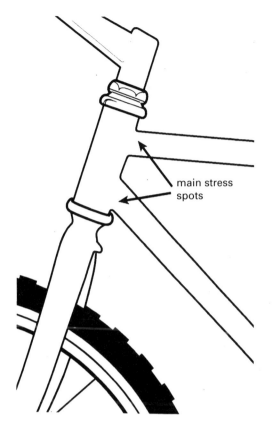

Fig 132   Make frequent checks for crash and general fatigue damage.

BRAKE MAINTENANCE
(Figs 133–134)

Brakes should also be checked regularly. Embedded pebbles, uneven wearing and unequal distance from the rim are all things to look out for. After some months or having ridden in extremely abrasive conditions, you should also check for wearing through to the metal stubs.

Toeing in brakes normally prevents the terrible squealing noise that they can make. A friend of mine found that his brakes still squealed after toeing in. Eventually he bought a brake booster (*see* chapter 8), which cured the problem.

The chances are that you will have Shimano brakes, as these are standard on some 70 per cent of all bikes. Regular balancing of the brakes' distance from

added reason not to let grime build up on the bike. If the paint on the main tube near the head-tube junction is looking creased or cracked, it should be scraped off to expose the metal beneath. If the metal appears cracked, the bike should not be ridden until the frame has been repaired or replaced. If the metal is not cracked, the surface should be repainted to prevent corrosion. Scraping paint off may sound rather drastic, but frame cosmetics are somewhat superficial compared with the prospect of being hospitalized after the frame has snapped at a bad time.

Fig 133   Toed in brake blocks. The trailing edge contacts the rim first. If the leading edge contacts the rim first the brakes will judder and squeal.

117

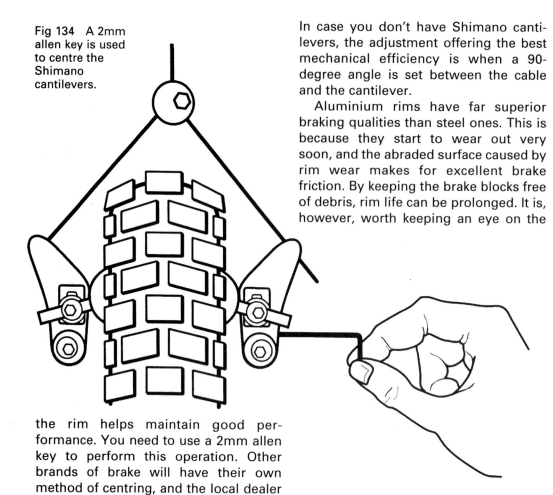

Fig 134 A 2mm allen key is used to centre the Shimano cantilevers.

In case you don't have Shimano cantilevers, the adjustment offering the best mechanical efficiency is when a 90-degree angle is set between the cable and the cantilever.

Aluminium rims have far superior braking qualities than steel ones. This is because they start to wear out very soon, and the abraded surface caused by rim wear makes for excellent brake friction. By keeping the brake blocks free of debris, rim life can be prolonged. It is, however, worth keeping an eye on the

the rim helps maintain good performance. You need to use a 2mm allen key to perform this operation. Other brands of brake will have their own method of centring, and the local dealer or mountain bike club should be able to advise with this.

When resetting brake blocks (sometimes called 'shoes'), care should be taken to ensure they do not contact the rim high (there would be a danger of wearing out the tyre), or low (they might dive under the rim when applied hard).

Periodic adjustment of the brake cable is also necessary. With Shimano brakes this can be a fiddly operation, and most good mountain bike dealers sell a cheap plastic guide to help set up the correct cable position for Shimano cantilevers.

rim wear. In an extreme case of neglect, a friend of mine wore his rims so thin that on braking hard the brake block went straight through the rim wall, and he was severely injured in the following crash. Inspecting the rims later revealed small wear holes. If he had checked his rims periodically, preventative action could have been taken. The rims had clocked up about 25,000km on road when this happened. A mountain biker might expect to wear rims out after as little as 7,000km off road in muddy terrain.

GEAR ADJUSTMENT
(Fig 135)

Like brake cables, gear cables also stretch. They stretch most when new, so you will normally have one or two adjustments to make within the first week of fitting new cables or buying a new bike. Incorrectly adjusted gears account for many of the problems newcomers to the sport have. It's easy to tell when the gears are correctly adjusted: the chain makes a quiet whirring sound as it passes over the rear cogs. If a clicking or clunking sound comes from the back as the chain is pedalled over the cogs, the chances are the gears need adjustment. Otherwise, something might be bent.

The cables can be adjusted wherever there is a barrel adjuster, or else they can be disconnected at the insertion to the derailleur mechanism and pulled tight with pliers before tightening the fastening clamp. Barrel adjusters are normally located on the lever and the derailleur.

The other important adjustment is to the hi/lo adjuster screws. These are indicated in the diagram, as is the rear derailleur barrel adjuster. The hi/lo adjusters prevent the chain from being derailed off the cogs or the chain rings

Fig 135 Hi/lo movement limits need adjustment when a new or different rear wheel is installed. Note also the barrel adjusters. They need regular tightening to keep the derailleur accurate.

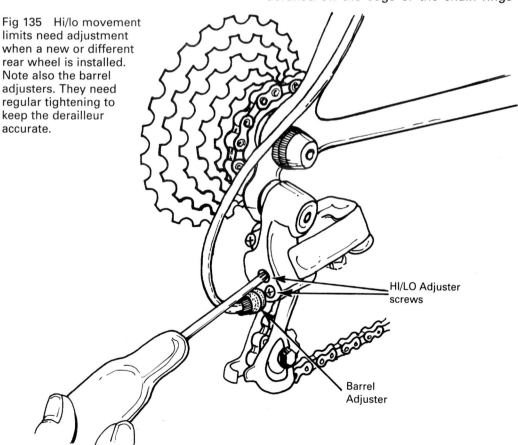

HI/LO Adjuster screws

Barrel Adjuster

altogether when changing to the biggest and smallest gears. Normally, these need to be set only once for a given wheel. As not all wheels are built the same, it is worth checking the hi/lo adjustment before the ride, rather than finding that the big cog is unobtainable or that the chain gets jammed in between the frame and smallest cog.

CHECKING THE HANDLEBARS

You should also check the handlebars for cracks. These would appear in the joint at each side of the head stem. If they are going to break, this is where they usually go. In seven years of mountain bike riding, I have not had a handlebar break, but with the ultra-light handlebars now available on the market, breakages are disturbingly common. I won't use any handlebar that weighs under 150g. Perhaps I err on the side of caution, but with the potential for serious head and spinal injuries that a front-end failure would involve, I have to question how important it really is to shave off those extra few grams.

QUICK-RELEASE SKEWERS
(Fig 136)

When I was fourteen, I learned something wonderful about the racing bike I had owned for a couple of years: I could release the wheel with a simple flip of a lever. For the previous two years I had been screwing the lever tight (and finding the system rather unsatisfactory, I recall) and loose. For me, this was a tremendous revelation, as used correctly the lever is a real time saver.

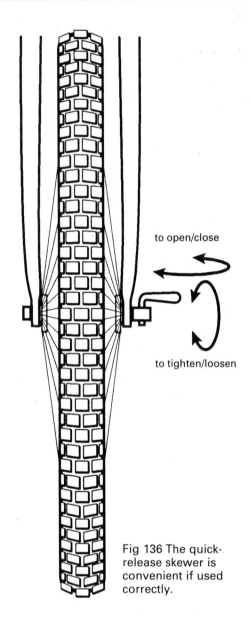

to open/close

to tighten/loosen

Fig 136 The quick-release skewer is convenient if used correctly.

The quick-release lever has two functions. It is screwed up until almost tight, then it is flipped over and a cam device effectively fastens the wheel into the frame. Quick-release levers have two main drawbacks, however. Firstly, they make it easy for bike thieves to steal wheels from bikes (so take care to lock wheels to the frame). Secondly, if not tucked away behind the frame tubes, they can be undone by flora along the track-side. You may not notice this until the front wheel comes loose going over a jump, but if carefully tucked in, this problem seldom arises.

NEW TUBES

It is a good idea to apply talcum powder to tubes before insertion. This helps to prevent snakebite punctures.

Between-Ride Maintenance
1. Clean bike.
2. Relube chain.
3. Check for signs of fatigue.
4. Make brake and gear adjustments with barrel adjusters.
5. Check where the tyre inserts to the rim for trail debris. No matter how small, this should be removed immediately.

Once-a-Week Checks and Jobs
1. Check tyre pressure.
2. Check brake cables and adjust brakes and gears as necessary.
3. Strip, clean and oil gear cables (never oil teflon-lined cables).
4. Check for loose screws, etc.
5. Clean and wax bike.
6. Check tyre sidewalls for damage (could be that the brake shoe is rubbing against the tyre).

Once-a-Month Checks and Jobs
1. Oil drum ends (lever attachment) of brake and gear cables.
2. Toe in the brakes.
3. Regrease head-set bearings (and wheel bearings if riding regularly in wet conditions).

4. Clean all traces of grime from all parts of the gears.
5. Remove and bathe the chain. Let it dry for a hew hours, then lube it thoroughly, wipe it clean and hang it up overnight before replacing it.
6. Clean all moving surfaces of front and rear derailleurs and brake levers (water displacing spray is good for this).
7. True wheels if they need it. If you cannot perform this vital skill already, start learning (instructions in Stevenson's book, listed in Further Reading).

Once-a-Season Checks and Jobs
1. Regrease bottom bracket bearings unless they are sealed units (this could be performed two or three times during wet seasons).

When to Seek Professional Assistance
1. Bent rims
2. Servicing suspension forks
3. Bent or cracked frame
4. Stiff spots in steering
5. Snapping spokes

TRAIL REPAIRS

Puncture

After removing the tube, don't let the tyre slide around the rim. This will help to locate the offending item if it is embedded in the tyre. Pump up the tube to find the leak. If it is not obvious, pump until it is. You can pass the tube in front of your ear to find a small leak. Match the position relative to the valve to find the cause of the puncture. Put in a spare tube.

If you don't have a spare, deflate the tube, stretch the area to be patched over the back of your hand and grip with your fingers to keep it taut. Thoroughly clean the area to receive the patch. This should be done with an abrasive. Sandpaper is good, as is a sharp edge. Rubber must be removed from the tube to be sure of adequate cleaning. Apply glue to the tube and smear it with your finger until there is only a very thin film, covering an area just larger area than the patch. Let the glue dry completely or else the patch won't stick. Apply the patch, and press firmly with your thumb for two minutes. Unwrap the tube from your hand.

If the leak is too big to patch, try isolating that section of the tube by folding it up and applying thick rubber bands to create an air lock. This actually works surprisingly well. I know a London cycle courier who worked for two weeks with such a repair in his tube (he couldn't be bothered to fix the tube properly sooner).

Taco'd Wheel

Tacoing a wheel means bending it like a banana. This looks as if it cannot be repaired, but an emergency straightening operation will usually return the wheel true enough so that it will revolve freely if the brake is unhooked.

Take the wheel out of the frame and place it flat on the ground. Two areas of rim, diametrically opposite, will be higher than the rest. Grip these two sections firmly and, kneeling over the wheel, quickly apply full body weight to the hands. The wheel should pop back into shape.

Cracked Frame

If the frame is cracked on the forks or near the head tube, start walking. If the forks are a little bent but don't catch on the main tube, it will be all right to ride gingerly – likewise with small frame folds near the head tube.

Snapped Rear Derailleur

If the rear derailleur is bent or broken to the point that the chain will not actually run through it, break the chain and remove the necessary number of links to bypass the damaged derailleur. The bike will have only one gear and if the chain line is not straight, the chain will frequently fall off. Choose a gear that will enable you to ride the remaining distance.

Broken Spoke

If the wheel is rubbing against the brakes, tighten the spokes on the same side of the wheel and adjacent to the one that broke. That will get you home. If this happens, you should take the wheel to a good wheel builder for a rebuild.

Glossary

Aerobic In the presence of oxygen.

Air/air time The distance a bike travels in the air when jumping.

Anaerobic In the absence of oxygen.

ATP Adenosine triphosphate. Muscles will not move without it.

Ballooner *See* **Clunker**. The difference is that ballooners invariably have very big tyres.

Bitchin' Of terrain: challenging or good fun.

Bonk/blow up To exhaust one's glycogen reserves, causing a feeling of enervation.

Bottom bracket The fulcrum of the bike, through which passes the spindle, or axle, joining the left and right crank arms.

Brazed A method of joining steel tubes by melting a thin brass strip onto the area to be joined.

Cadence The rate of pedal revolutions, normally per minute.

Centre tread/ridge A tyre pattern creating a virtually uninterrupted central line of contact with the road surface.

Clunker A heavy, unwieldy and inefficient bicycle. Also refers to the original Marin County mountain bikes.

Cluster The group of gears attached to the rear wheel.

Dart A long, narrow knob pattern on a tyre, giving excellent traction around corners.

Derailleur The mechanism used to derail the chain from one cog to another. The bike has two gear derailleurs: one for the front gears and one for the rear gears.

Detonate To exhaust one's glycogen reserves, as for bonk, etc.

Dropped In racing, left behind.

Drop off A large step on a trail, can be ridden down or up.

E Stays See **Elevated stays**.

Elastomer A springy synthetic material used in suspension forks. Said to be better than air/oil over small bumps.

Elevated stays Raised chainstays to eliminate chain suck.

Endo When the front wheel suddenly stops causing the rear wheel to go in the air, sometimes ejecting the rider over the handlebars.

Gnarly Rough surface, normally combined with a steep slope; difficult riding conditions.

Granny ring/gear The small inner chain ring of a triple chainset.

Hardpack Trail with a particularly firm surface.

Highside The bike is flipped outwards and sideways by centrifugal force as it turns a corner.

Knobblies The heavily treaded mountain bike tyre.

Lactate Also called lactic acid, a by-product of the oxidation of glucose with insufficient oxygen.

Lactate tolerance The capacity to which muscles can continue working in the presence of high concentrations of lactate.

Lactate system The energy system in which lactate is produced, cleared and converted. Includes anaerobic glycolosis.

Lube (d) Short for lubrication or lubricate.

Mech (Front or Rear) Another common name for the front and rear gear derailleurs. *see* **Derailleur**.

Metal matrix composite A new class of metals introduced by the space and arms industries. Essentially MMCs, as they are known, use complex processes to integrate particulates, such as silicon carbide or boron, into materials such as aluminium in a way that produces a reinforced metal.

Monocoque A frame made not with joined tubes, but one piece of material – normally carbon fibre.

Off the front Leaving one's racing company behind.

Oversized A term normally relating to frame tubes. Lighter and thinner frame material can be used by increasing the tubing diameter. Such tubing is now standard on mountain bikes and is known as 'oversized' tubing.

Ovalized Frame tubes are sometimes squashed to an oval section at certain junctions. This increases the rigidity of the frame.

PCr Phospho-creatine, also called creatine phosphate.

Phosphate battery The quantity of ATP and PCr that is very quickly available to fuel muscle activity, but is depleted after only a few seconds.

Ring One of three cogs comprising the chainset, to which the cranks and pedals are attached.

Shreddin' Riding very fast when clearly on-form.

Slicks Mountain bike tyres with no tread made for road use.

Smoked Outpaced.

Smokin' Riding very fast.

Snakebite A two-pointed puncture caused by an impact in which the tube is squashed between the rim and an external object. The walls of the rim actually puncture the tube.

Taco'd When a wheel is bent to resemble the edge-on-view of a potato crisp.

Transmission The chainset, chain, gears, rear hub, and freewheel.

The sage Hardy desert or grassland flora of more than one genus.

Travel The amount of movement in a suspension system.

Wheelbase The distance between front and rear axles. Short wheelbases can turn in tighter spaces, but long wheelbases offer more stability at speed.

Wipeout Spectacular crash.

Useful Addresses

CLUBS AND MAGAZINES

Australasia

Australian Cycling Federation
68 Broadway
Sydney
NSW 2007
Australia
Tel: (02) 2818688

New Zealand Cycling Association
P.O. Box 35-048
Christchurch
New Zealand
Tel: 3851422

Cycling World
200 Crown St
Darlinghurst
NSW 2010
Australia
Tel: (02) 3315006

Great Britain

Countryside Commission
John Dower House
Crescent Place
Cheltenham
GL50 3RA
England
Tel: (0242) 521381

British Mountain Biking Federation
36 Rockingham Rd

Kettering
Northants
NN16 8HG
England
Tel: (0539) 412211

Scottish Cycling Union
Meadowbank Stadium
London Road
Edinburgh
EH7 6AD
Scotland
Tel: (031) 652 0187

Welsh Cycling Union
4 Orme View Drive
Prestatyn
Clwyd
LL9 9PF
Wales
Tel: (0745) 85272

Rough-Stuff Fellowship
Belle View
Mamhilad
Pontypool
Gwent
NP7 8QZ
Wales

Cyclists' Touring Club
69 Meadrow
Godalming
Surrey
England
Tel: (0483) 417217

Off Road Cycling Association
Raycombe Lane
Ledbury
Herts
HR8 1JH
England

MTB Pro, Mountain Biking UK
30 Monmouth St
Bath
BA1 2BW
England
Tel: (0225) 442244

Mountain Biker International
9 Dingwell Ave
Croydon
CR9 2TA
England
Tel: (081) 686 2599

Cycling Weekly
Kings Reach Tower
Stamford St
London SE1 9LS
England
Tel: (071) 261 5588

North America

National Off-Road Bicycle Association
1 Olympic Plaza
Colorado Springs
CO 80909
USA
Tel: (719) 578 4596

Canadian Cycling Association
1600 Promenade James
Naismith Drive
Gloucester
Ontario K1B 5N4
Canada

International Mountain Bike Association
4359 Pampas Rd

Woodland Hills
CA 91364
USA

Mountain Bike Hall of Fame and Museum
P.O. Box 845
Crested Butte
CO 81224
USA
Tel: (303) 349 7382

WOMBATS
P.O. Box 757
Fairfax
CO 94978
USA
Tel: (415) 459 0980

Velonews
1830 North 55th St
Boulder
CO 80301 USA
Tel: (303) 440 0601

Mountain Bike
33 E. Minor St
Emmaus
PA 18098
USA
Tel: (215) 967 5171

Mountain Bike Action
10600 Sepulveda Boulevard
Mission Hills
CA 91345
USA
Tel: (818) 365 6831

South Africa

South African Cycling Federation
P.O. Box 4843
Cape Town 8000
South Africa
Tel: 557 1212

Further Reading

Background Material

Countryside Commission CCP186, *Out in the Country* (1985)
 Cycling in the Countryside (1987)
Oliver, T., *Touring Bikes: a Practical Guide*, The Crowood Press (1990)
Sidaway, R.M., *Good Conservation Practice for Sport and Recreation*, Sports Council, Countryside Commission, Nature Conservancy Council, World Wide Fund for Nature.
White, F.R. & Wilson, D.G., *Bicycling Science*, MIT Press (1982)

Practical Advice

Cotton, N., 27 'Places to go – tried, tested, legal and decent.' *Mountain Biking UK* magazine; Spring Special.
Edwards, S. (n. d.) *The Heart Rate Monitor Book.* VeloNews Books (n.d.)
Evans, J. *Offroad Adventure Cycling.* The Crowood Press (1990)
 50 Mountain Bike Rides, The Crowood Press (1993)
Fleming, J. *The Well Fed Backpacker.* Random House (1985)
Hackett, P. *Mountain Sickness (Altitude)* American Alpine Club (1986)
Horten, H. *Cycling Off-Road and the Law.* Cyclists Touring Club and Bicycle Action (1987)
National Park Foundation. *The Complete Guide to America's National Parks.* Washington DC (1984)

Palmer, C. *Offroad Cycling Trail Guide.* Offroad Cycling Association (1992)
Snowdonia National Park. *National Voluntary Cycling Agreement – Snowdonia* (1992)
Stevenson, J. *Mountainbike Maintenance.* Springfield Books (1990)
Walker, K. *Wild Country Camping.* Constable (1990)

Serious Reading for Enthusiasts

Bollen, S. *First Aid on Mountains.* British Mountaineering Council (1990)
Bunelle, et al. *Cooking for Camp and Trail.* San Francisco: The Sierra Club (1984)
Gallwey, W.T., *The Inner Game of Tennis*, Pan (1986)
Jannsen, P., *Training Lactate Pulse Rate*, Polar Electro OY, Oulu, Finland (1987)
Langmuir, E., *Mountaincraft and Leadership*, The Scottish Sports Council (1984)
McNeill, C. *Orienteering: The Skills of the Game*, The Crowood Press (1989)
Pedgley, D.E. *Mountain Weather: A Practical Guide for Hillwalkers and Climbers in the British Isles.* Cicerone Press (1979)
Syer, J. and Connolly, C., *Sporting Body, Sporting Mind*, Cambridge University Press (1984)
Watts, A. *Instant Weather Forecasting.* New York: Dodd Mead & Co (1968)

Index